The reminiscences of Chief-Inspector Littlechild

John George Littlechild

The Making of Modern Law collection of legal archives constitutes a genuine revolution in historical legal research because it opens up a wealth of rare and previously inaccessible sources in legal, constitutional, administrative, political, cultural, intellectual, and social history. This unique collection consists of three extensive archives that provide insight into more than 300 years of American and British history. These collections include:

Legal Treatises, 1800-1926: over 20,000 legal treatises provide a comprehensive collection in legal history, business and economics, politics and government.

Trials, 1600-1926: nearly 10,000 titles reveal the drama of famous, infamous, and obscure courtroom cases in America and the British Empire across three centuries.

Primary Sources, 1620-1926: includes reports, statutes and regulations in American history, including early state codes, municipal ordinances, constitutional conventions and compilations, and law dictionaries.

These archives provide a unique research tool for tracking the development of our modern legal system and how it has affected our culture, government, business – nearly every aspect of our everyday life. For the first time, these high-quality digital scans of original works are available via print-on-demand, making them readily accessible to libraries, students, independent scholars, and readers of all ages.

old books. new life.

The BiblioLife Network

This project was made possible in part by the BiblioLife Network (BLN), a project aimed at addressing some of the huge challenges facing book preservationists around the world. The BLN includes libraries, library networks, archives, subject matter experts, online communities and library service providers. We believe every book ever published should be available as a high-quality print reproduction; printed on-demand anywhere in the world. This insures the ongoing accessibility of the content and helps generate sustainable revenue for the libraries and organizations that work to preserve these important materials.

The following book is in the "public domain" and represents an authentic reproduction of the text as printed by the original publisher. While we have attempted to accurately maintain the integrity of the original work, there are sometimes problems with the original work or the micro-film from which the books were digitized. This can result in minor errors in reproduction. Possible imperfections include missing and blurred pages, poor pictures, markings and other reproduction issues beyond our control. Because this work is culturally important, we have made it available as part of our commitment to protecting, preserving, and promoting the world's literature.

GUIDE TO FOLD-OUTS MAPS and OVERSIZED IMAGES

The book you are reading was digitized from microfilm captured over the past thirty to forty years. Years after the creation of the original microfilm, the book was converted to digital files and made available in an online database.

In an online database, page images do not need to conform to the size restrictions found in a printed book. When converting these images back into a printed bound book, the page sizes are standardized in ways that maintain the detail of the original. For large images, such as fold-out maps, the original page image is split into two or more pages

Guidelines used to determine how to split the page image follows:

• Some images are split vertically; large images require vertical and horizontal splits.
• For horizontal splits, the content is split left to right.
• For vertical splits, the content is split from top to bottom.
• For both vertical and horizontal splits, the image is processed from top left to bottom right.

THE REMINISCENCES

or

CHIEF-INSPECTOR LITTLECHILD.

The Reminiscences

OF

John George

Chief-Inspector Littlechild.

"Fiat Justitia ruat coelum"
"Let justice be done though the heavens should fail"

1894.
LONDON: PUBLISHED BY

The Leadenhall Prefs, Ltd: 50,-Leadenhall Street, E.C

Simpkin, Marshall, Hamilton, Kent & Co., Ltd.

New York   Charles Scribner's Sons, 743 & 745, Broadway.

THE LEADENHALL PRESS, LTD LONDON, E C.
(T. 4658)

TO POSSIBLE CRIMINALS

I DEDICATE this Book to those who, having within them the germs of crime, are in constant danger of falling into its dark abyss, and if every such person will purchase a copy, ample remuneration awaits my labour. If the perusal of its pages should cause but a small number to "look before they leap," my reward will be greater. If one truth stands out more prominently in my experiences than another, it is that "The way of the transgressor is hard"

CONTENTS.

CHAPTER   PAGE

I.   I Introduce Myself   1

II.   An Agony Advertisement   13

III.   How the Diamond Mail was Robbed   25

IV.   Tracking a Forger   35

V.   How the Turf Frauds were Discovered   45

VI.   The Russian Gold-dust Swindle   55

VII.   My Pet Criminal   66

VIII   How I have used Disguises   76

IX.   How I Discover Clues   85

X.   Betrayed by a "Copper's Nark"   95

XI.   Breaking up a Sham Loan Office Gang   104

XII   Mistaken Identity and its Dangers   116

XIII.   Companions in Crime   127

XIV.   How Forgers Baffle Detectives.   138

XV.   A "Plant" upon Pawnbrokers   149

XVI.   Capital, Ten Shillings   159

XVII.   Captures made at Sea   169

XVIII.   Mr. Borrowdaie's Sapphire Ring   179

XIX.   A Fraud upon Freemasons   189

XX   Why Men have "gone wrong"   200

XXI.   A Superstitious Criminal   209

XXII   More Coincidences in Crime   219

XXIII. And Last.   A Ghostly Adventure   227

REMINISCENCES

OF

CHIEF-INSPECTOR LITTLECHILD.

———◦◦◦———

CHAPTER I.

I INTRODUCE MYSELF.

"ON the Grampian Hills my father fed——" Well, as I am writing my personal detective experiences and not a biography, it matters not where my father fed his flocks; or, for the matter of that, whether he had any flocks to feed—other than geese   Why, or wherefore, I "donned the blue" and, with "a truncheon by my side and a helmet on my brow," patrolled the streets, the admiration of nurse-maids, who love the coat if not the man, and sport of little boys, who would peep round corners, at a safe distance, and cry, "Mother, be proud of your boy in blue," there is no need here to relate.   I was very young then, and could not tell why I did many things.   I remember how amused I was at being told on the first day I went to learn drill that I must shave, no hair being permitted on the upper lip in those days.   I really had no idea myself that I had any hirsute adornment to take off, and felt somewhat proud that some one else seemed to think I had; but the next moment I felt very foolish, as I fancied the drill instructor was just "getting at me" on account of my youthful appearance, which I thought was very much against me, as my idea of a policeman was that he should have big side whiskers and a gruff voice, and I had—neither! But, when in the course of a few months I was selected for certain detective duties, my youthful appearance, instead of being a source of annoyance and a drawback, was all in my favour, as I shall presently narrate.

It does not fall to the lot of every man to drop into a profession, or calling, suitable to his taste or to which he is, or thinks he is, suited, even where much thought and discussion have been bestowed upon the subject by fond mothers and more or less practical fathers. The whole thing is a conundrum, and many a man would be better off to-day had he been left to his own choice

In this respect I have certainly been fortunate, and have always congratulated myself on the fact that the life of a detective was suited to me in every way. I have often heard the saying that every man thinks he could "edit a newspaper," "run an hotel," make an actor, or be a detective.

I could not edit a newspaper, neither could I run an hotel, and from experience am sure I have not in me the makings of an actor, but I certainly have striven very hard to leave on record some evidence of having been a detective.

The love of adventure and of excitement has always been strong within me, and hence it is that the life of a detective has been so congenial. The ever-varying changes in the daily duty, in scene and incident, the uncertainty of movement and lack of monotony that necessarily attaches to the career, and the excitement that must be present with even the coldest and most unimaginative of natures, have had a charm for me which not many other callings could have afforded

There is something interesting that may be written in every man's life, and I have been forcibly struck with this truth when reading in my official capacity the outpourings of certain criminals who, as is frequently the case, write a kind of biography in a confessional or "getting-square-with-the-conscience" kind of way I have invariably read these literary efforts, generally of very illiterate men, with interest, and this fact prompts me in a great measure to place some of my own experiences on record in the present form.

It must not be supposed from these remarks that the life of a detective is all a bed of roses. Far from it, especially in what may be termed the apprenticeship days, when much of a man's time is taken up in tedious and laborious watching, frequently during many hours at a stretch, for days and weeks together—much of it fruitless, and nearly all of it irksome—and, moreover, a detective is often compelled to walk as many miles during a day as a country packman, without the chance of taking a meal.

A great part of a detective's work is necessarily done by night, and many of his experiences while on the alert for a "burglar when he's burgling" are calculated to shake his nerves—ludicrous though they may often be when traced down to the first cause. For example, during the early days of my plain clothes work I had a good sound fright which I can afford to laugh at now, but did not then.

I was engaged in watching a house in the outskirts of London at night. The house stood in its own grounds and was removed from any well-frequented road. So large was the private park that one might imagine one's self to be in the country.

It was a fearfully dark night—the darkness might almost be felt—and appeared to threaten a storm. No one in the place knew that I was watching it.

I was armed with a dark lantern, and I knew the grounds pretty well. The owner, who was a much-travelled man, had erected a museum in them, which was stored with casts of heathen gods, stuffed alligators, snakes, and such creepy things. This museum was under my observation as well as the house

My hiding-place was amongst the laurels, and of course I kept perfectly still, making no noise. Presently I fancied I heard a sound which was unusual, so I cautiously crept out and stole to the museum. Something prompted me to turn my bull's-eye light into it, and its rays suddenly flashed upon the hideous array of objects, gleaming ghostly amidst the shadows. My blood fairly ran cold upon beholding these horrors. You must know that it was then two a.m., and I was perfectly alone in the stillness of the place. Withdrawing my fascinated gaze from these ghastly relics, I retreated towards the house, bent upon discovering the cause of the stealthy noise which had attracted my attention.

There was a terrace to the mansion, and the French windows of the drawing-room opened upon it. Every fastening appeared all right, when again I heard the strange sound.

Instantly I turned round and flashed my light.

Then, in a moment, there was the noise as of the rushing of many waters—a roaring of Lodore, and simultaneously something white started up. It was in front of me upon the lawn. My blood froze in my veins; I lost all command of myself, and I stood transfixed My heart seemed to stop beating, and my breath ceased.

In a little while this paralyzed condition left me, and I was able to collect my thoughts. I turned to ascertain the cause of the mysterious sight and sounds, my lamp shining brightly, when, as I moved, there was a renewal of the fearful rushing as of black-winged fiends slipping past me. I cannot give a better description. To tell the truth I was horribly frightened, but it occurred to me that the volume of sound was less than before. Suddenly in a flash an explanation of these startling phenomena occurred to me. Of course it was very simple. The white visions which I had seen were so many statues of goddesses which were placed on pedestals, and which were suddenly thrown up in relief when my bull's-eye was turned upon them. The lantern had also served to scare hundreds of sparrows, which had been perching in two large hawthorns, and it was the beating of their wings which had produced the rushing noise that to my excited nerves had filled me with awe.

Of course duty of the foregoing nature was intermixed with work of a far pleasanter and more social character. Well do I recollect the part which I played in the suppression of certain betting houses in the West End. It was at the period when the night resorts of the metropolis were being put down. These were the days of Kate Hamilton and the heyday of Panton Street and other streets in the neighbourhood of the Haymarket The old landmarks have disappeared, and names which were once familiar are now forgotten—Jack Coney and Kate Hamilton among the rest !

It was the Early Closing Act which dealt the deathblow to many of these rendezvous, especially to such of them as were licensed, but other dens, where liquor was sold, as it is sold in bogus clubs to-day, were kept in full swing for a while, until certain facts came to the knowledge of Sir Richard Mayne, then Commissioner of Metropolitan Police, and he determined to cleanse the Augean stable To that end he advised very rigorous measures to be taken; and the employment of police-officers who were utterly unknown to the frequenters of the West End places was a matter of urgent necessity, each of the night houses being guarded by a cordon of touts and spies on sentinel duty. It was not an easy thing to run the gauntlet of all these gentry in order to gain admission, unsuspected, to the premises Frequently a suitable introduction was necessary, and all manner of stratagems were used by the hawks of the establishment to satisfy themselves that strangers admitted would not be likely to give information to the police. It was a part of my duty, of course, to invent various tales about myself to allay their curiosity, which afforded me much amusement, but I knew very well that it was my willingness to be plucked which made me an acceptable visitor rather than their belief in my assertions that I was " Captain Jinks of the Horse Marines."

Some dissipation was inevitably associated with the part that I played, but, although the hours were late, the time was a pleasant one The results were highly successful, although my private purse suffered. I acquired much knowledge which was useful to me in after days, and which led to prosecutions being made under the excise laws. The imposition of heavy fines broke the night houses up.

Thus, with varied duties   perform, I spent the early days of my detective career,   inning, as all my colleagues have done, at the lowest   of the ladder, and passing through successive grades t   rank of Chief Inspector.

The reminiscences which   related in this volume are those chiefly connected with what may be termed ordinary, as distinct from political crime. I have striven to avoid repetition, for necessarily much of the experience whi   have gained presents features of similarity. My aim has been to select cases in which the criminal has hit upon some new idea, or original plan, which, in turn, has demanded exceptional skill on the part of the detective to bring the crime home to its perpetrator

One unpleasant experience was common in my younger days, which I trust is less frequent now. I allude to a bullying cross-examination on the part of a certain class of Old Bailey barristers. They were very few, and I doubt if such men exist nowadays. Their maxim was, "No case, bully the detective," and I have never lost an opportunity of having a cut at them in return. One of the old school, long since gathered to his fathers, started to cross-examine me as to the exact spot in the Strand where I had arrested a notorious coiner. "Now," said he, "which side of the Strand was the prisoner on when you first saw him? Was it the east side?" "No," I replied quietly, immediately detecting the topographical error. "Was it the west side?" he demanded   "No," said I, quite unmoved.

Then he started to rave. "What do you mean, sir? Do you know you are on your oath? You said just now you first saw this man in the Strand. What do you mean by it, sir? Which side of the Strand was it you saw him?" "The south side," said I, and down he sat, the whole court indulging in a laugh at his expense, the judge included.

This kind of "brow-beating" rarely benefits a prisoner. As I once heard Mr. Commissioner Kerr say of young barristers, "They generally manage by their cross-examination to convict their clients."

The later years of my service at Scotland Yard were in connection with the "special" branch of the Criminal Investigation Department. I was its chief inspector, and it fell to my duty to arrest many dynamiters and to be brought into contact with men whose names stand out prominently in the history of the "physical force' policy, adopted by the extreme wing of the Irish party, and which began in this country with a mild, though unfortunately fatal, explosion at Salford Barracks on January 14, 1881, and ended, practically, as far as London was concerned, with the breaking up of the dynamite conspiracies in the Jubilee year, 1887.

At this period—Colonel Howard Vincent, C.B., who for some years was Director of Criminal Investigations, having left us, much to our general regret—Mr. James Monro, C.B., was Assistant-Commissioner, and the late Mr. A. F. Williamson Chief Constable. Two better chiefs, in my opinion, are not to be found in any police force in the world. Their praises have been so constantly sung, but I could not allow these reminiscences to go forth without paying a tribute to the memory of Mr. Williamson, whose faults were few and virtues many, and whose name I shall always revere, in common with every detective of his day.

Mr. Williamson required knowing. Strangers, when they entered his office, were apt to form the impression that he was heavy and unimpressionable; but they soon changed their opinion, for, no matter the intricacy of the case submitted to him, he immediately gripped its points, and required but ten words of explanation when others asked for fifty. He was always most courteous, and he had the faculty of inspiring confidence in the most timid—a rare qualification in a police-officer in these days. The dictatorial tone is by far the more common one, and many are the ludicrous instances when a step down from the pedestal has had to be taken, and the manner adopted which should have been taken from the first.'

Williamson was full of dry humour, which frequently came out in the anecdotes which he enjoyed telling.

On Sunday mornings, when the gatherings at the office were in the nature of a friendly conference, when the work which would not wait till the morrow had been got through, then he would come among us, and many a pleasant hour can be recalled of these Sunday mornings by my old colleagues, of whom, I regret to say, too few remain.

One day, he used to say, he was in Brompton Cemetery, attending the funeral of one of the old officers. Having seen his subordinate placed in his last resting-place, the day being fine, he walked about among the graves almost aimlessly, noting the inscriptions on the tombstones and in a reflective mood generally, when he came upon a labourer doing up a grave. The man, though advanced in years, was tall and well set up, and Mr. Williamson, fancying that he recognized him as an old pensioner, said to him as their eyes met—

"Halloa! don't I know you? Weren't you in the police force once?"

"No," said the man. "Thank God I have never sunk so low as that yet."

Williamson was practically born a policeman, his father being the superintendent of T (Hammersmith) division. He spoke French well, and applied himself to learn German after he was forty years of age, which forcibly illustrates the kind of man he was. He took an active part in the suppression of Fenian conspiracies during the outbreak of 1866 and 1867, when the explosion occurred at Clerkenwell prison; but, strange to say, he held the majority of Fenian conspirators and their conspiracies very much in contempt.

An informant once came to him and in all seriousness gave the startling information that some Fenians were practising cavalry tactics in Jerry Flannigan's back kitchen in Theobalds Road. This was too much for Mr. Williamson's gravity, and it was with difficulty he could take a serious view of Fenianism afterwards. Nevertheless it did not deter him from giving careful attention to what was going on from time to time.

As years rolled on all those officers who had obtained a knowledge of Fenian conspirators had either died or left the service, and in 1880, when the first rumblings of fresh troubles were heard, I was instructed by Mr. Williamson to take up the matter as a special study, and every point calling for inquiry was referred to me. The lack of previous knowledge concerned me not at all, as the conspiracy business was to a certain extent under new management.

Most of the men who had taken part in the '67 movement had retired or gone over to the majority. But I reserve the narrative of my work in this connection for another occasion, for—as Mr Rudyard Kipling would say—that is "another story."

I would, however, here express my opinion that there was a wide difference between the movement of '67 and the dynamite campaign with which I had particularly to do. The former was undoubtedly a Fenian "rising," popular among all Fenians, and having the avowed object—abortive though it proved—of making a strike for Irish independence Many of the attempts then made were simply fiascos—the intended raid on Chester Castle on February 11th, 1867, to wit, yet other events demonstrated the determined spirit of some of the leaders, as, for instance, the attack on the police van in Hyde Road, Manchester, on September 18 of the same year, made with a view to the rescue of two notorious prisoners—Colonel Kelly and Captain Deasy—accused of treason felony. On that occasion, it will be remembered, Sergeant Brett lost his life. A more disastrous outrage still was that committed at Clerkenwell House of Detention, when the wall was blown up by means of a barrel of gunpowder, and some of the houses in the neighbourhood deprived of their fronts, leaving them like "so many dolls' houses"—as Williamson used to say—"with the kettles still singing on the hobs." Here, again, the object was the attempted rescue of a prisoner—Colonel Rickard Burke—although, strange to say, had he been in the exercise yard at the time that the explosion occurred, as the conspirators anticipated, he must have been killed. As it was, twelve innocent people were done to death.

But as regards the 1881–89 period, of which I shall have hereafter to speak in detail when I pen my memoirs of these troublous years, there was no intention of making a blow for independence. Certainly the patriotic element which no doubt animated the '67 rising was absent from the dynamite campaign. I know that many tried and trusted Fenians held entirely aloof from it, and the instigators of the Physical Force Movement took very good care not to risk their freedom and their lives by crossing the Atlantic. They left that portion of their diabolical work to be done by their tools and agents. It makes me shudder to think of the consequences if these emissaries had been successful in all their operations. That more lives were not sacrificed is to me marvellous The public does not realize the peril in which it was placed It was indeed fortunate that detection dogged the steps of these desperadoes, and that their arrest followed so surely upon their crimes. The part which I played in this connection forms an interesting chapter in my history. Terrorism was the object of this later movement, in order to compel legislation in a desired direction, but that terrorism reckoned without its host. Evil-doers rarely give Scotland Yard credit for efficient policing; so much the better for the public good.

Absorbed as I have been in what may be called the circumventing of the "isms" of crime, still I must admit that the expert forger, the ingenious swindler, and the inventive genius of roguery are each and all very interesting studies—more so, perhaps, than the tool of the dynamitard —and it has therefore been a pleasant task to put upon record some of the methods which I adopted to bring these gentry to justice, as these experiences will show.

CHAPTER II.

AN AGONY ADVERTISEMENT IN A MORNING PAPER, AND WHAT CAME OF IT.

" DEAR F.,—I implore you to give me help in this my hour of deepest trial   Friendless and ill, I can look to none but you. By the memory of the happy past I entreat your aid, or I know not what I shall do.   My last shilling will pay for this advertisement   O remember me at this season of re-union   I have no home now, so please address G.C., care of X , Fleet Street "

Such an advertisement appeared in the Agony Columns of more than one leading newspaper; so on the face of matters "G.C.," whoever she was—the advertiser was apparently a lady—had enough money left to make known her appeal to "Dear F." in a fairly systematic and rather expensive manner.

Now, as it may be guessed, the Agony Column is studied as closely by the detective police as by any one, and this advertisement attracted my attention. To most people, I suppose, it would read as the genuine heartfelt production of a young woman abandoned in the Great City at Christmas time by the person she addressed as "Dear F." —heartless lover or faithless husband ?

There are numbers of charitable people in the world who would readily help a really deserving woman in distress, and it occurred to me that possibly this advertisement might be directed to lightening the pockets of the injudicious giver. Of course, the appeal might turn out to be a *bonâ fide* wail of a forlorn girl, and in that case it would not concern me in a professional sense.

In my early days the rule at Scotland Yard used to be if there was no complaint made, or no prosecutor to come forward, to refrain from interference with men who were obvious swindlers. The fear was that the liberty of the subject might be imperilled, and the rogues and thieves took full advantage of this reluctance to upset our boasted English freedom.

But when Mr. Howard Vincent became Director of the Criminal Investigation Department he, with great courage, would direct the initiation of prosecutions, or the breaking up of gangs of swindlers where prosecutions could not be obtained for the want of some person to take proceedings

I had no difficulty, therefore, in getting permission to make inquiry respecting the "Dear F." advertisement.

First I paid a visit to X. in Fleet Street—it was simply a place where letters were received—and there I was informed that for some time a young woman had been in the habit of calling for letters.

She had received a great many.

"Does she come frequently?" I asked.

"Pretty well, but I have not seen her for the last two days," said the shopkeeper. "She is a nice-looking girl, and appears to be in great trouble."

I thought my theory was falling to the ground. However, just to be thorough, I went to the offices of the newspapers which had published the advertisement, and was permitted to see the "copy," or manuscript of it.

I was amazed at the discovery which I then made. The handwriting was not that of a girl, but of a man; moreover, I knew that man well, and at that time was watching him narrowly in consequence of certain suspicions which I had formed respecting his movements.

In fact, this man, a Parsee, with an associate, had been called as witnesses at my instigation to prove that certain advertisements were inserted in provincial papers respecting a loan-office business which had been started as a genuine concern, but which had degenerated into an inquiry-fee extorting bureau, and finally collapsed on the appearance of the principal in the dock.

These witnesses, who were to prove the insertion of the advertisements, were a most extraordinary pair—shifty and unsatisfactory in every way.

When I walked with the one the other would say—

"Just be careful of X.," indicating his friend, "for he is a queer lot," and his companion would express himself similarly, but with more Oriental courtesy, in regard to the other man, on the next occasion when he was alone with me.

The reason for the extraordinary reluctance of these men to appear in the witness-box I soon afterwards discovered.

The past history of the Parsee and of his partner fully explained their aversion to come publicly to the front in a court of law. Many of the Indian gentleman's doings no doubt did not bring him within the scope of the criminal law, but they had culminated in his arrest and that of his associate, and subsequent sentence to a term of imprisonment, a fact of which I was ignorant when first I made their acquaintance, and which naturally they did not desire that I should know.

When the Parsee first came to England he was possessed
of a literary and social ambition, which he had not the
capacity to gratify. In some way he made friends with a
gentleman, who told me this story—

"I happened to have on paper a number of translations
of Indian poems, which I had made in the midst of
linguistic studies, and some of these one day I showed to
my Parsee friend. He cajoled me into giving him the
permission to publish these verses as his own, under the
title of 'Pearls of the Peri,' and he commissioned me to
make other translations for him, saying that his native
name would guarantee their genuineness. I must confess
that I was partly influenced by a desire to see what critics
would say of my efforts, as I had some idea of publishing
poems of my own afterwards."

"Pearls of the Peri" served the Parsee very well, for the
book gave him some sort of footing in the journalistic
world. He dabbled in newspaper work in various ways,
and during the whole period he was also obtaining money
as a begging-letter writer, setting forth in these appeals that
he was a starving young poet from India, and that the
purchase of a copy of his "Pearls of the Peri" would give
him bread.

Another of his ideas was to insert in the newspapers an
advertisement of this type —

"A FORTUNE can be gained by persons of either sex, without
any risk or outlay   Success is certain to whoever tries   Full
particulars on receipt of eighteen stamps."

In reply to the applicants who sent the necessary stamps
the Parsee would forward on a printed slip a moral receipt
for making one's fortune .—

"Waste not, want not. Save every penny and waste not a moment."

Many similar advertisements were being "worked" at that period, indicating that it was a lucrative business, and the Parsee was living in clover as a country gentleman upon the proceeds

So far he had succeeded in evading the law, but he now concocted a scheme which possessed novel features.

His first step was to take offices near to a well-known firm of publishers, and next to adopt a trading name closely resembling theirs. At this address the Parsee and his partner republished " Pearls of the Peri " under a new title, and they then sent throughout the country to booksellers a number of prospectuses of the book. Each circular was enclosed in an envelope sealed with a coronet and directed in a lady's hand. A coronet was embossed upon the letter paper, and the note written thereon purported to have been penned by a Lady T——, and ran —

"Lady T——, at the recommendation of her friend, the Countess of Z——, would like the book named in enclosed prospectus to be obtained for her as soon as possible. On her return from town in a few days she will call and pay for it "

Many booksellers, upon the faith of this order, wrote to the publishers for copies at half a guinea apiece and sent remittances.

Of course, Lady T—— never put in an appearance to claim the poems, and the books were left on the hands of the too-confiding shopkeepers.

In the result the enterprising publishers were prosecuted, and as it was proved that " Pearls of the Peri " was worthless and unsalable, they were convicted and went to prison.

c

Now when I saw that the handwriting of the advertisement addressed to "Dear F.' was that of one of these very smart publishers, I surmised that it was a new dodge to catch the unwary, but the *modus operandi* was not quite apparent. There was, however, distinct encouragement to proceed

My plan was to obtain the permission of a well known society to advertise in its name, repeating a portion of the "Dear F." appeal, and requesting any person who had replied to it to communicate with the secretary of the society.

The replies received were handed to me, and I then waited upon the writers. Some of them had been deceived into the belief that the agony advertisement was the genuine outpouring of a wronged woman's heart, and had sent money without making inquiry, yielding to the impulse of sympathy.

Others had asked "G.C.,' the advertiser, to call upon them, and "G.C." came. The motives of some people who invited her, I am sorry to say, were open to question

"G.C.," after all, was not my Parsee friend, the unwilling witness, but an apparently respectable young lady, quiet in demeanour, and described to me as looking very pale and ill.

"My father," said she to her new-found friends, "was a magistrate in the North of Ireland, but he died a year ago and left me an orphan. His property had been left jointly to my brother and myself. My brother was trustee, and he squandered it.

"I fell into straitened circumstances, and I married an officer of high rank in the army. But he has deserted me, and I now believe my marriage to him was illegal, but I am making this last appeal to him, for he has left me no address. He is no longer in the army."

The girl sobbed pitifully as she told this tale, and coughed from time to time. She raised a handkerchief to her lips, and when she removed it it was slightly stained as with blood. She seemed desirous of concealing this symptom of lung complaint.

Such evident distress of mind and weakness of body produced its immediate results. "G C." — "Grace Chalmers" was the name given by her—invariably went away with money and offers of help.

Of course it was possible that Grace Chalmers might have told a true tale, but I was puzzled to account for her association with the man I had known, and whose handwriting I clearly identified as having written the original of "G.C.'s" advertisement in the Agony Column.

Chance has often favoured me in my detective work, and it did not fail me in this instance.

Among those who had obtained an interview with "G.C." was a gentleman whose motives I have every reason to believe were honourable although that is more than I can say of many of the other men who had replied to her advertisement.

Whilst I was interviewing this young gentleman who had seen and helped Grace Chalmers, a letter which had come by post was put into his hand.

With a smile he handed it to me.

It was from Grace Chalmers herself, and in it she asked him to meet her at a particular time and place, as she wished to see him urgently. It was a complete surprise to this gentleman to receive such a letter, as the girl had refused his offer of a situation in a large West End house, on the plea that she could not accept it as her "dear mother" had dealt there. He certainly never expected to hear from Grace again.

However, at my suggestion the gentleman agreed to meet Grace Chalmers, and I dictated to him a cautious reply to her letter, which he wrote and sent to her.

On the following morning he kept the appointment, and so did I.

The girl's object, I afterwards learned, was to satisfy herself whether the gentleman who had so kindly assisted her had seen the advertisement which had run counter to her own, and she told a plausible story that it emanated from a person who wished to do her an injury. She begged him—her friend, as she called him—to take no notice of it.

They parted, and I then "shadowed" this interesting young lady to her abode. Certainly in appearance she was no swindler, although for that matter I am no believer in what are called criminal looks. Thieves are not to be distinguished from ordinary people, except, perhaps, the pickpocket when he is at work, at which time he is often painfully nervous, and betrays it by the quick movement of his eye.

Nevertheless, I arrived at the conclusion that Grace Chalmers was not the dupe which I had considered her to be. In fact, I now believe that, instead of her having been the tool of the man who wrote out her advertisement for her, she had, to some extent, deceived him even by her plausible and affecting story.

Very early the next day I was, with assistance, at the house to which I had traced Grace Chalmers.

"Is Mr. X. in?" I asked the servant, giving the name of my friend the unwilling witness.

"Yes," said the girl.

"Drawing-room floor, isn't it?" I hazarded

"Yes," said the girl again

"Don't bother," I said, "to ask him down I'll go upstairs to him."

And, with a second officer closely at my heels, I bounded up the staircase.

I knocked at the drawing-room door

Miss Grace Chalmers, in deshabille and appearing very much astonished, opened it.

We pushed unceremoniously into the room, and her look changed to one of dismay.

Mr. X. sat at breakfast, and he stared at us blankly, with his mouth full—for he had lost the power of swallowing his food.

"Good morning," I said. "Sorry to disturb you at breakfast."

"Good morning, Mr. Littlechild," the Parsee answered mildly, as though he had expected me.

"You will guess the object of this early visit," I continued. "I am about to arrest this young lady on various charges of fraud in connection with the 'Dear F' advertisement, and to ask certain explanations of you."

"I am not guilty, and she is not guilty of fraud," said the man. "It isn't fraud to help a fellow-creature in distress."

I did not argue that point.

Grace had asked permission to retire to her room, and she was allowed to do so, precautions being taken to prevent her escape, and when she returned she had made a wonderful change in her appearance. She was "dressed to kill."

She was not the first woman whom I have known, in somewhat similar circumstances, to rely upon what is usually termed a "prepossessing appearance." It had stood her in good stead once before.

I remember one case—that of a woman who was brought before the late Sir James Ingham at Bow Street Police Court neatly and quietly dressed.

The magistrate took a kindly view of her case, and allowed her to find bail. When she again appeared at the court upon the second remand she had, for some reason, put on her fine feathers.

Sir James looked at the prisoner in astonishment, and, in his usual good-humoured way, said—

"Is there not some mistake, inspector? Is this the young woman who was before me last week?"

The solicitor who represented the prosecution smartly said—

"Yes, Sir James, this is the same young lady. But she is in her war-paint now."

To return to Grace Chalmers.

A number of letters from people who had sent money were found by us in the house, which went to show that the advertisement in the Agony Column had realized large profits.

As Grace Chalmers steadfastly refused to give any information in regard to herself, I made inquiry into her history, and I found that it did not at all correspond with the pitiable story which had so moved the hearts of the benevolent public.

The only clue to her antecedents was afforded by a remark which she made to a lady, that her father lived in the West of Ireland. She alleged that he was a magistrate.

I went to this district, and after much inquiry discovered that Grace had been employed at a shop in a small town, and that she had been charged with theft by her employers. She had been tried at the assizes, and she asserted that the stolen goods were perquisites; and such was the susceptibility of an Irish jury that her prepossessing appearance in the dock led to her acquittal.

"Sure, sor," exclaimed the foreman to one of the counsel afterwards, "such a good-looking colleen would niver have taken the things at all!"

Grace, although acquitted, felt her character was gone, and she drifted to Dublin, and there adopted a pretty name. She had a craze to become an actress, and met with a man who represented that he was connected with the stage, and offered to get her an engagement. Ruined by him, she went from bad to worse.

I felt the profoundest pity for her father, who was a good and worthy man. He had served in the Papal Zouaves, and had gone through the troublous times preceding 1848, when Pius IX. was compelled to fly from Rome. He was a fine specimen of an old soldier.

To the last Grace Chalmers preserved the most perfect effrontery, and never quailed when she was sentenced to imprisonment. I had hoped that when I confronted her with her innocent sister—a lovely girl, whom I had brought from Ireland—the sight of her fresh pure face would have caused the wicked woman in prison to abandon her bold demeanour; but she still adhered to her story, and remained loyal to the Parsee, by whom she had been infatuated. This miserable man allowed her to take the full responsibility of the crime, and she met her punishment undismayed.

It may be asked "But was not the girl really ill? Did she not stain her handkerchief with blood?"

Yes, she did; but the stain was not that of blood. She had been chewing betel-nut.

CHAPTER III.

HOW THE DIAMOND MAIL WAS ROBBED—"FROM INFORMATION RECEIVED."

EVERYBODY in South Africa recollects, I dare say, the daring robbery of £70,000 worth of rough diamonds which were in transit from the Kimberley diamond-fields to England. But how that robbery was planned, and in what manner it was effected, it remains for me to disclose, and in so doing I now make considerable use of "information received."

It happened that a very clever organizer of criminal campaigns was a few years ago travelling in South Africa, "partly on business, partly on pleasure," as he said, and in course of his journeyings he found himself in the companionship of an American sneak-thief at Kimberley.

Now, at that period Kimberley was not connected by rail with Cape Town, distant about 650 miles, nor, all the way, with Port Elizabeth (Algoa Bay), about 480 miles off. The mail from the interior to the coast was carried by coach to the nearest railway station, involving a journey by road of over 400 miles across the country.

The coach started every fortnight, and carried with it parcels of diamonds which were being conveyed through the post-office from the mines to England.

It was not to be supposed that the mode of transporting the precious mail from point to point passed unnoticed by the unscrupulous rogues in whose earlier career nefarious dealings with diamonds had more than once figured

"Bill," said his leader, known as the "Boss," addressing the sneak-thief—"Bill, we can't afford pleasuring any longer; we must get to business."

"Right you are, guv'nor; but what is the lay?"

"Diamonds, Bill, diamonds!" and the eye of the "Boss" glistened

"Should hev thought you had had enough trouble over them, Boss."

"Oh, you mean that Paris job. I was a bar keeper then, wasn't I, Bill? Yes, it was B——'s bar first of all—he started it after we cleared the Boston National Bank of half a million dollars (£100,000) in bonds But he took to drink and gambling and dropped most of his share I had a mortgage on the property, and for everybody's sake I foreclosed and entered into possession."

"Curse him," muttered Bill beneath his breath, "the Boss gets the better o' all of us!" He then added aloud—

"And that was when you tricked the diamond merchant."

"Quite so, Bill. It was neatly done. The fellow used to hang about my place with the intention of catching the Yanks. He carried with him a case of gem jewellery, worth, I should say, £8000. I bought several things of him and recommended him to my customers. In fact, I told him to call from time to time, and the fellow was only too pleased to come."

"What a spider you are, Boss!" exclaimed the sneak-thief admiringly; "the chap came once too often."

"He did I put up a job to have his case stolen whilst he was in my bar. One day I got him into conversation deep, and whilst his back was turned Jimmy, an American lad, simply walked off with it. You should have seen the dealer's face when he first missed it. 'It's stolen!' he cried, 'my diamonds are gone!' 'Nonsense,' said I; 'there's nobody been in the bar since you've been here to day.' 'But I showed you the case when I came in,' he urged. 'You did *yesterday*," I replied, 'but not *to-day*. I don't recollect your bringing the case this morning at all!'"

"That was a clever move o' yours," commented Bill "I recollect what followed. The dealer didn't own the goods himself, but was merely a commission agent for a Paris house. They had him arrested, and he was in prison for several weeks. Weren't you up before the judge yourself, Boss?"

"Yes, many times; but I always stuck to the story that the dealer didn't bring the case to my place and must have left it elsewhere, and the end of it all was that the chap got so frightfully mixed that he couldn't swear for certain that he had brought the diamonds to my bar at all. Ha, ha, ha!"

"If the police had known as much about you as we do, Boss, they would have arrested you on the spot."

"Perhaps so," said the "Boss." "As it was, we comfortably disposed of the swag, some months afterwards, in New York."

"And it was after that, Boss, we did the little job together of lightening the Calais train of 700,000 francs in Egyptian and Spanish bonds, wasn't it?"

If these worthies had been permitted to have continued their reminiscences I do not know to what extent they might not have thrown light upon the biggest jobs in the way of bond robberies which have taken place of recent years I have reported so much of their conversation to show that one of the pair, at all events, was a most dangerous man I confess to having watched him myself with the closest attention, whilst he has lived in London, and I owe the following story of his South African crime to the information placed at my disposal by one who knew the "Boss" well.

I am inclined to believe, myself, that this genius went out specially to the diamond-fields to prospect for this particular job, and it will be seen with what patience and at how great an expense the arch-rogue perfected his plans

Now, on his road from Port Elizabeth to the diamond-fields the "Boss" had first of all observed that the mail-coach was, at a certain point of its journey, conveyed across a beautiful broad river, which was too deep in the wet season to be forded For this purpose a flat-bottomed ferry was used, and the boat in question was attached to a wire-cable, by which it was enabled to journey from bank to bank.

"I wonder," said the "Boss" reflectively to his pal, the sneak thief, "what would happen to the boat if the cable broke."

"Or was cut?" hinted the other darkly

"It would probably float down stream," continued the other, and then, as though speaking to himself, he added, " and cause delay, and delay is all that we want."

Nothing more was said, but, arrived at the diamond-fields the conversation took place between the two men which I have above reported, and as the result of it they set quietly to work to make themselves fully acquainted with the mode of conveying the mail, with the diamond parcels, from the interior to Port Elizabeth. When they had posted themselves up in all the details, the "Boss" stated his intention of returning to the coast, and on the homeward run by coach his companion noticed that he took special observation of the manner in which the wire-cable to which the ferry-boat was fastened was carried from shore to shore.

But the "Boss," who was the man of brains, did not disclose his ideas fully to his subordinate. The time for such confidences had not arrived, as other men were required for the job.

At Port Elizabeth the "Boss" exclaimed, "And now for the postmaster!"

The postmaster was a genial sort of man, and it was not difficult to make his acquaintance. Further, during a stay of several weeks, the thieves wormed themselves into his confidence, until at last they were permitted to roam as they pleased about the private part of the premises, and even obtained access to the room in which the safe was kept.

"Bill,' whispered the "Boss" one day to his confederate, "to-night I shall make myself particularly agreeable to my friend the postmaster, you understand, and shall take him out to have a drink. We shall leave you behind—you'll be too lazy to join us. Whilst we are away just see if you can't get an impression of that safe-key."

"I'm fly!" agreed Bill

That evening the postmaster and the "Boss" went out drinking, and the sneak-thief obtained what his chief required—a mould of the safe-key in wax.

"When do you go back to England?" asked the post-master casually of his friends.

"By the next steamer," the "Boss" answered, and by the next steamer they both went.

There dwelt, at the time of which I am writing, a gentleman of means in a suburban house, and this individual was accustomed to make at intervals Continental tours, some of them of a rather prolonged character.

Returning from one of these peregrinations, this highly respectable suburban householder gave a dinner-party to his friends in very good style. I rather fancy that the police would have been pleased to have been present at that little festivity, for their eyes would have been opened somewhat

The host was none other than our friend the "Boss," and his guests included not only his sneak-thief travelling companion, Bill, but two other gentlemen in the same branch of the profession, who had graduated by "doing time"

"Now, gentlemen," cried the "Boss" of the gang after dinner, the servants having withdrawn from the room, "the plan that I have to lay before you promises to pan out well. My friend Bill, who was with me at Kimberley, and also at Port Elizabeth, can assure you that it is no gammon—there's diamonds worth £50,000 to divide if there's a penny. The question is, will you trust me?"

"Yes," they shouted in chorus.

"Well, then, friends, what I shall want you to do is to abide explicitly by my instructions. You, Jack, and you, Jem, must stop in Port Elizabeth, and hang around till you hear from me. It won't do for either Bill or myself to be seen in that quarter, for we are too well known. What you have to do is to watch for the mail which brings the diamonds from the fields They will be locked up in the safe, to wait for the next vessel, and in the mean time the safe must be 'cracked'—do you understand?"

"Hold on a bit, guv'nor, why won't there be a vessel in waiting for the mail?"

"You leave that to me. I'll take care the mail steamer shall have left before the coach arrives at the station nearest to Port Elizabeth You won't have any difficulty about the safe."

"We shan't, eh, Boss?"

"No, because here is the key, or a fac-simile of it, which is almost the same thing"

The gang gave vent to their admiration of the high qualities of organization displayed by their chief, who took their praise as though it were his due.

Soon afterwards the company dispersed, and each man travelled to Africa by a different steamer, Bill and the "Boss," however, going together. They posed as ostrich-feather dealers, and on their arrival they purchased a two-horse team and drove up the country for over two hundred miles

"Say, 'Boss,' we ought to be near that river now!" said the sneak-thief, after much wearisome travelling.

"You are right, Bill. We shall soon be with my brother and his wife."

"What have they got to do with it, Boss?"

"They are just staying hereabouts for the benefit of their health, Bill," replied the "Boss," with a sharp look in his

eye; and then quickly added, "You dullard! Do you
think it would have done for the two of us to have been
seen loitering about here and run the chance of being
recognized by people we met before. No, I looked ahead;
and that was why my brother and his wife came out to
Port Elizabeth a month or two ago. They have a house
on the river, and in that house we shall be put up until the
mail comes along, and nobody will be the wiser."

"You're a cute one, Boss," said Bill, and he relapsed
into silence as the team jolted down the uneven road which
crossed the drift, leaving a tangle of wood behind them,
and on each side passing huge boulders scattered amidst
the coarse reedy herbage on the margin of a shallow stream.

At last they came to the river.

"There's much more water than there was when we were
here last," commented Bill.

"Of course," quietly responded the "Boss." "It is the
rainy season. That is what we have been waiting for."

"Look here, Boss," said Bill, "I'm still in the dark.
What do you mean to do?"

"You ought to know by this time, Bill. Do you think
that river is too deep to ford?"

"Yes; and the stream runs too strong."

"Could they drive the mail across it?"

"No; but there ain't no need, the mail will be on the
ferry."

"No, it won't, because the ferry-boat won't be there."

"Snakes! Blest if I didn't think you meant to cut the
cable and let the mail drift down stream, Boss."

"No, Bill, it's safer to let the boat drift without the
mail, and keep the coach waiting on the other side. All

I want is delay. Now, supposing the mail is kept waiting twenty-four hours until the boat is towed back, what will happen? It will be a day late on the railway, a day late at Port Elizabeth, and the steamer *can't wait*. The diamond parcels will be taken to the post-office. Jack and Jem are there; they have the key, and they will take the swag—that's the idea!"

"Captain, you are a genius!"

By this time it was evening. The two scoundrels went to the house which was occupied by the brother of the "Boss," and this man was able to inform them that the mail was expected to arrive the next morning.

In the dead of night the "Boss" slipped out of the house and made his way unseen to the ferry. No time was to be lost. He hacked away at the wire cable desperately, and at last it parted. Away swept the boat down the stream, and when the morning came, and with it the mail-coach from Kimberley, the boat was fully eight miles off.

There was a hue and cry for the ferry, and when the missing boat was found it had to be towed to its former position, in order that it might bring the delayed coach over to the other side.

In this way the mail was kept on the wrong bank of the river for a whole day, and, as the chief conspirator had foreseen, when the journey was resumed on the other shore and the railway terminus reached, a special train even failed to arrive at Port Elizabeth in time to catch the steamer for England.

The mail-bags were therefore placed in the post-office, and in due course, a few nights afterwards, the diamond parcels mysteriously disappeared from the safe

D

Of course the postmaster was suspected, and he was arrested, but no evidence could be given against him on that charge

It may be imagined that the thieves lost no time in bringing their booty to London, but it was not their plan to hurry matters, and it was not until some months had passed before this transfer was made

Diamonds are not easy things to sell, and the quantity for disposal in this case was so large that extraordinary steps had to be taken by the gang One of them was installed in an office not far from Hatton Garden, in partnership—as diamond merchants—with the man called the " Boss."

The pair had studied the business of diamond dealers very attentively, and in the result they were successful in selling the stolen stones to the very persons to whom the diamonds had been originally consigned !

CHAPTER IV.

TRACKING A FORGER—A CHASE IN TWO CONTINENTS

£200 REWARD !—WANTED, on a Warrant for Forgery, MARK MERTON, late of, etc , etc

Mark Merton was a clerk employed by a very large firm, and he had embezzled about £10,000 upon a highly ingenious plan.

In connection with the business a savings bank had been instituted, and Mark Merton was its secretary, doing the work after office hours He was a sober, quiet, highly respectable man to all appearances, but he had been unable to resist temptation.

During five years he had "cooked" the accounts of the savings bank in a systematic way. To each depositor was issued a pass-book, which had to be sent periodically to the auditors The fraudulent secretary kept a double set of leaves to these books, and when the audit was due he would unstitch the deposit books and remove the leaves, replacing them with others which agreed with his ledgers. When such manipulated books were returned to Merton duly initialled, he would take out the substituted leaves and return to their place the pages which were originally in the covers and which recorded correctly the transactions of each depositor. He would cast up the totals, calculate the interest due, and forge the auditors' initials.

In this manner Merton was able to deceive the depositors on one hand and the auditors on the other, with a double set of books, having a single set of covers.

It must have involved a great deal of trouble, and sooner or later there was bound to be a crash

One day it came.

A depositor happening to be at the auditors' office when the audit was in progress, inquired in mere curiosity the amount of his savings The total which the clerk named was so much less than the sum he had actually lodged with the bank that his astonishment was great. Inquiry was set on foot. Bank Holiday intervening, nothing could be done until Tuesday, but on Wednesday morning the secretary wrote to his firm—

"I have no wish to escape the punishment of my offence, and I simply go away because I dare not face you, or any one else, to explain, nor can I ask for pity."

In a word, the bird had flown I was summoned, and the bill offering £200 reward for the capture of Mark Merton was put into my hands.

But where in all London—nay, in all England, with more than fifty-eight thousand square miles to hide in—was I to find my man? He had simply walked away from his home, but whither? There was no clue beyond the end of the street.

Mark Merton, I discovered, had been living handsomely, and had become very popular in his neighbourhood, for he always figured at the head of subscriptions for church and charitable purposes.

Occasionally he would ask leave of absence for a few days and go away On his return to the office he would appear in mourning and a hatband, and very confidentially he would say—

"Ah! poor Uncle John has gone at last. A good fellow —a good fellow—he did not forget his pet nephew."

Thus most people thought Merton was able to live so well because of these periodical legacies—for when it was not Uncle John it was Aunt Mary, or some other rich relation, who had bequeathed him money.

And it was by this fiction that Merton accounted for his comparative wealth.

Now, in working out this case I reflected that Mark Merton would probably keep in touch with some relation or intimate friend, and it occurred to me that in most families there is usually a member who is generally looked to for advice, or gives it without asking, upon all matters of small moment, or of difficulty In an emergency the aid of such a person is summoned

I therefore kept my eye open to discover the existence of the family oracle—aunt or uncle, or oldest friend, as the case might be. We found such a gentleman—for he was a man and not a woman, and we—my colleague and I, as there were two of us in the case—watched him narrowly. I must say this "shadowing" gave us an infinitude of trouble

A detective does not often have to employ horses in carrying on "observation," but our friend—the oracle—had an awkward habit of trotting off in a pony trap, and if he were not followed on those occasions, he might have taken any step to deceive us.

At last, however, by a variety of ways—by waylaying servants, by sly inspection of postmarks on letters which were delivered at the house, and by taking advantage of every small scrap of information—we believed ourselves to be in possession of knowledge pointing to the ultimate intentions of the man whom we were systematically following.

We therefore relaxed the "shadow," and then, apparently, dropped it, for it soon became clear to us that our quarry believed that the chase had been abandoned. Of course this delusion exactly suited our purpose.

Our pursuit had led us up and down the country, and finally to Liverpool, where one day the gentleman whose movements had interested us so greatly walked into a shipping office and took certain tickets for America

It was sufficient for us; and very soon two more tickets were obtained for my colleague and myself. My companion it was necessary should accompany me, as he was able to identify the man we hoped to make our prisoner—the missing Mark Merton.

Mark Merton's friend—the family oracle, whose movements to this stage we had successfully traced—had booked his berth by a slower liner than the one we had selected. His ship was a four-wheeler, ours was a hansom, and we calculated we should arrive at our destination three or four days ahead of him

Fortunately I was able to catch a mail which was in front of us, by which I wrote to my friend, Mr. T. Golden, of New York. We were old chums, for he had spent with me three months in England, in connection with a heavy case of forgery, involving a sum of three hundred and twenty-five thousand dollars, and I had had the satisfaction of seeing him off at Liverpool, with his prisoner and much of the money

Great was my disappointment upon landing not to meet Golden, but just as I was beginning to despair I recognized him, bearing down upon us under the shadow of a great green umbrella—for it was a very hot day.

I felt that success was assured, but having seen the Chief of Police and the British Consul, I was a little damped. The latter informed me that my case would be taken up by the United States Marshal, to whom all extradition matters are transferred

Golden had tried to discourage me from calling upon the Consul, and I understood his reason when I found that I was handed over to a young gentleman who came into the Marshal's office in his shirt-sleeves, with hair dishevelled, and a cigar between his teeth He sat himself familiarly down, crossed his legs, exposing the frayed ends of his trousers and his well-"ventilated" boots, and my heart sank within me as I looked at him.

"What," thought I, "is my case to end in failure after all these weary months?"

I bewailed my bad luck to Golden when we left the office together.

"Never mind," said he, cheerily. "We'll pull the wool over his eyes. I will look after this case"

Tim Golden was as good as his word, and he never deserted me.

On the arrival of the vessel which brought the family oracle and friend of Mark Merton into port, we were ready to take up the shadowing again; but we had to be very careful, as my London colleague and myself were both known by sight to this gentleman

It was arranged that Golden should alone appear. His appearance was that of a fine-looking man, somewhat over middle age, wearing gold-rimmed glasses and carrying a green umbrella He walked slightly lame, and this limp, with his military moustache, suggested that he had fought and bled in the Civil War.

I may say we had sent the Marshal's man home to his mother—or dinner

My London colleague and I were both stowed away in a small wooden shed on the quay. which was stored with old rope, tar and barrels There was one window, which gave a view of the road which the passengers who were to disembark from the steamer must take, but we could not see the ship itself

There were the hope and chance that Merton the forger would meet his friend on the quay The risk and danger of our being seen through the window were very great

The sun was pouring upon the roof of the shed, and we were nearly suffocated with heat and blinded with perspiration.

Whilst we were thus cooped up, intent upon watching every person who passed from the ship, Golden meantime waiting for the signal to take up the following, a hat-box was suddenly placed on the sill outside our window, right in front of my eyes.

At once I saw that the man who had put it there was our friend the oracle, the very individual we were expected to point out to Golden.

There he stood just outside our window, but fortunately with his back to it

Down we dodged amongst the ropes, the tar, and kerosene, but we were not seen. We squeezed out of the back and succeeded in giving Golden the signal.

Another curious thing happened

For a very long time we waited for Golden, who was following the oracle, to return When he rejoined us, he told us that this gentleman had selected our hotel at which to stop Of course we could not go back to our rooms, and our mysterious disappearance was never explained. Golden, however, paid our bill for us, sent us our luggage, and remained in the hotel to watch

On the following day another narrow squeak of recognition occurred.

The luggage belonging to the oracle was that afternoon to be fetched from the ship I had seen it myself in the early morning on the quay. As I was walking with the British Consul—on my way to get, if we could, the contents of a telegram which we had ascertained had been despatched by the oracle on the previous day upon landing, probably to Merton himself—I noticed a cart. I saw the hinder part only, but recognized one of the trunks I had inspected that morning.

Looking round to discover whether the cart was being followed in our interests, and seeing no one, I grew alarmed, and ran after the vehicle to make sure of the trunk

But, whew! On the front of the cart sat the gentleman who had blocked my vision with his hat-box on the previous day.

I was nonplused.   It was madness to run after a trotting horse in a broiling sun to an unknown destination, and if it happened that the man in front of the cart should turn and see me, all would be discovered.   It would be equally absurd to allow the cart to go without tracing it

In this dilemma I looked around, when, in a vehicle which was following, I saw the beaming face of Golden

"Bravo, Tim!" I cried.

"All right, my boy," he replied, "just you become invisible, right away."

I lost no time in putting as many "blocks" of houses as I could between myself and the cart, which Golden meanwhile followed.

Golden tracked the luggage to its destination, and next morning we all three were up early, Tim going ahead to "spy out the land"

In less than two hours Tim returned, his face beaming like the setting sun, and with something in his gait which told of success.

As Pat would put it, "the first thing he said was to shake hands."

"You have good news!   Out with it, old man."

"You are right, my dear boy," Golden replied.   "Our fish is landed, and I don't think he is at all sorry for it, as he looks as though he had had enough of hiding."

As Merton told me himself, he really did experience relief when he was arrested, for the suspense had been torture, and many times he had been on the point of surrendering himself, but he had been unable to muster up sufficient courage.

Without a character he had been unable to find employment, and he had walked about the streets frequently hungry He had contemplated turning organ-grinder, and a piano-organ had actually been purchased in England for him.

After the usual extradition proceedings had been observed, my prisoner was committed to take his trial in this country, and the usual seventeen days' interval having elapsed—which I much enjoyed as a rest—Merton was handed over to me.

Some people say a detective can always be told by his looks I do not believe it

On the return voyage I obtained permission for my prisoner to accompany me into the saloon for meals, enjoining the captain and purser—who alone knew who he was—to strict secrecy, as I did not desire to have attention called to myself.

However, it became bruited abroad—perhaps because one of the passengers recognized me—that there was a Scotland Yard detective with a prisoner on board.

Oddly enough, as we sat in the saloon with my prisoner on my right, on my left was a gentleman whose father had been brutally murdered some few months previously An ugly rumour spread—for which there was no foundation—that this young fellow had been guilty of his father's death

Opposite to me sat an Englishman with whom I had become acquainted. We often paced the deck together, and he said to me one night—

"Halloa! have you heard who the man on your left at table is?"

I told him that I had, and he continued—

"I hear, too, there's an inspector from Scotland Yard on board"

"You don't say so," said I. "I wish you would point him out to me. I should like to see one of these Scotland Yard fellows"

"Oh," he replied, "I don't quite know him yet, but I think I have found him out I'll show him to you soon'

"Do," said I, and shortly afterwards, meeting a man on deck I imagined would realize his idea of a detective, I asked, "Is that the inspector?"

"No," said my friend, "he is not the man I take to be him"

Next day I was watching the porpoises gambolling, when my friend leaned over my shoulder and said, in a very cautious and comically confidential way—

"I say, Mr Littlechild, you have been given away on this ship."

"What do you mean?" said I, hardly able to refrain from laughter, but he was so serious

"Oh, it's no use now," he replied "I know who you are Your name is too well known"

And we both had a hearty laugh

CHAPTER V.

HOW THE TURF FRAUDS WERE DISCOVERED—A STRUGGLE FOR LIFE.

APART from dynamite conspiracies, and explosions, and the Whitechapel murders, perhaps no matter has been regarded of such great importance at Scotland Yard as the discovery of the Great Turf Frauds of 1876 It was my lot to play a considerable part in their detection They are the theme of much tradition at Scotland Yard, and before I proceed to my revelations it will be desirable that I should, for the information of the younger generation, lightly sketch the nature of this gigantic imposture, drawing upon my memory for its outlines.

The promoters of the scheme had profited by the experience of earlier rogues in the same line of business, and determined that it was essential they should command the assistance of a man possessed of journalistic powers and the ability to speak French. They decided that it was not necessary that such a man should be informed at the outset that he had joined a gang of swindlers, and the business in hand was to be conducted in such a way that to an outsider everything would appear to be open and above board.

To obtain the journalistic genius required, the prime movers adopted the ordinary plan of advertising

The advertisement caught the eye of a man who for unscrupulous cleverness, was more than the match of any member of the gang who proposed to employ him.

Of course I refer to the notorious Henry Benson. This man, after the Franco-German War, had represented himself as the Mayor of a French town and obtained £1000 from the Chief Magistrate of the City of London—part of a fund raised at the Mansion House to relieve sufferers by the war Benson was convicted of this fraud, and upon his liberation from prison (in which he had endeavoured to commit suicide by making a fire of his clothes in the cell and sitting upon them) he went to the Isle of Wight. There he became the proprietor of a newspaper, but as it was not altogether prosperous he accepted the position offered to him by the Turf Fraud gang.

Briefly, the object in view, on the face of it, was to "break the bookies"—i e victimize the bookmakers attending race meetings for betting purposes—by a system of what may be termed "moral certainties."

Benson's duties were thus defined. He was to edit and contribute articles to a bogus newspaper, which was to be published in England and in France with the purpose of extolling the wonderful methods of a certain man, whose successful betting had become so well known that leading bookmakers held aloof from him.

The newspaper contained general news concerning sport, and prominently advertised the names of "certificated" or "registered" bookmakers—the fact being that there was no such thing as a register for betting men , but this title was adopted to give colour to the transaction, especially on the Continent, where such a system does exist.

The head of the gang very soon perceived that their new editor was as "ily" (sharp) as himself, and confidences were exchanged, with the result that Benson became a partner and moving spirit in the game.

Benson was of good education and culture, his father having been a man of position in Paris.

The newspaper was circulated assiduously in France among the class of persons who were likely to come within the scope of future operations.

To selected addresses letters were directed following up the newspapers, and these letters purported to have been written by the marvellously fortunate backer of horses. In effect these communications stated that as he had met with such great success and the bookmakers would no longer deal with him in consequence, he desired, therefore, some responsible person to act for him in forwarding his cheques to certain bookmakers. This agent would receive the winnings and remit them to the backer, incurring no risk by the transaction.

Bogus cheques, I should say, were printed in readiness.

Into this trap a very large number of people fell, and consented to act as agents to the Fortunatus of the Race-course.

It was explained to them that the method adopted by him was not to lay money on big races, in which the chances were more uncertain, but on smaller events, in connection with which his facilities for information were sure. This proviso was intended to get over an initial difficulty, for the results of leading races are always "wired" to France, but of the lesser ones nothing whatever is known abroad, and, therefore, purely fictitious race meetings could be put forward and played upon by the gang

Immediately a person consented to act as agent, a bogus cheque was forwarded   him with instructions to remit it to a certain bookmaker resident at an address covered by one of the swindlers   ing him to back a certain horse for a certain race.

In due course a letter would arrive from this bogus book-maker enclosing a cheque, which was worthless, represent-ing the imaginary winnings   This cheque was returned to the backer, who would send another cheque representing a second bet, and so the game went on until the agent, burning with the desire to make money for himself, or herself, would remit a sum to be put upon a horse by the fortunate and well-informed backer in London

Of course this was exactly what the gang desired, and they held out inducements until the victim was pretty heavily enmeshed in their toils, when he would be fleeced by a "big scoop," and then the correspondence would cease

In this manner the gang netted £10,000 from one lady alone, and would probably have obtained more if her banker, suspecting fraud, had not obtained her permission —she was very indignant at the proposal—to wire to Scot-land Yard for information concerning her correspondents.

The reply was brief   " The scheme is a fraud "

Until this point the conspirators had acted very cleverly, but then came the false step which a criminal invariably makes

The swindlers went to Scotland and changed the £10,000

into Clydesdale Bank notes, for, as these notes are not numbered, they believed that they could not be readily traced, but it never occurred to them that, as this Scottish paper was in such small circulation in England or abroad, it would afford a better clue to the detective than ordinary Bank of England notes could.

Scotland Yard soon became very busy, for having made £10,000 at one haul, the gang broke up and dispersed.

The game would otherwise have gone merrily on, for dupes losing small sums, under £200, might never have thought it worth while to complain and become the laughing-stock of the public. The disposition to " grin and bear it " is often the characteristic of victims of the " confidence trick," and the Turf Frauds, after all, were only a new version of this well-worn dodge.

I fancy that the desire for great gains easily acquired, when it takes possession of a man, makes him temporarily insane. I cannot otherwise account for the fact that the smart Yankee is usually the most frequent prey of confidence-trick rogues. When they come to their senses, men who have been " done " often concoct ludicrous and amusing stories to account for the loss of their money, which they come to Scotland Yard to report   But the practised officer soon detects the deception, and enjoys the foolish look which spreads over the face of the romancer.

It was very soon suspected that the prime mover in the Turf Frauds was a certain individual, but he had been sufficiently 'cute not to have shown himself in any way which would have enabled us to fix his share in the transactions.

He seemed to have no fear of us; but this man became

E

the object of my care and attention, when our suspicions
were confirmed by the discoveries following the first arrest,
which, I may state, was effected in consequence of "information received."

The man who gave this information had been asked to
cash a £100 Clydesdale note, and no doubt he thought
that, as there was evidently something irregular in the
transaction, he could do better by giving information to
Scotland Yard than by buying the note. He had arranged
to meet the man who had the note for sale at S^t. Martin's
Church, Trafalgar Square

At the appointed hour I was there too, with Inspector
Robson, and after keeping the individual who held the
note under observation for some time, we took him into
custody, and this was the first arrest in connection with the
great Turf Frauds.

When an arrest once takes place in a case, developments become rapid   The caution so necessary when the
detective is feeling his way is to some extent removed.
There is a French proverb "It is a wise man who knows
when not to speak." Applying the rule to detective work,
I would say, "It is a wise officer who knows when *not*
to make inquiry." One can be too precipitate in these
matters, but having made your first capture, there is
generally no time to lose in completing your case.

In many instances there is more detective skill required
in connecting the links of a chain of evidence than is
necessary to effect an arrest.

The first capture having been made, then it was that I
began to "shadow" the suspected principal of the gang,
and as I knew the man well, and also his haunts, I had no

difficulty in "picking up" the trail, but the subsequent watching was indeed laborious.

My chief object in all this observation was to discover whether others engaged in the fraud, whose descriptions I had, would join their leader and especially whether Benson, the man who had done newspaper business and French correspondence, we an interview with him.

Other officers were meanwhile engaged in following up the faintest clue, but the great hope of the police was that the extensive circulation of the information concerning the Clydesdale notes would yield something to work upon These particulars were sent not only throughout England, but scattered broadcast over the Continent

Benson and two other men belonging to the gang had decamped to Rotterdam, and, believing themselves secure, they began spending their notes. Already the landlord of their hotel had formed his suspicions, and had compared the description of the man "wanted" with Benson, so that when the latter asked him to cash a Clydesdale note he was satisfied There was not much difficulty about the identification, as Benson was very lame as the result of his burns when he had attempted martyrdom at the stake in Newgate.

The Rotterdam police were called in, and all the men were arrested and extradited. Meanwhile evidence was accumulating against the suspected principal, and on the evidence in hand—a person having been found in the course of inquiry who could identify this man in connection with the chief address from which the gang had carried on their operations—a warrant was obtained.

This warrant was placed in my hands for execution. For a few days previously my observation had been relaxed purposely to allay suspicion. Personally I was very thankful for the rest, for to tear about after this man, who frequently drove a smart horse and trap, with my eyes fixed upon him, often in the most disadvantageous circumstances, was no joke or easy matter, especially when he would be up and down the course, and in and out of the ring, at some race meeting, for the matter did not spoil his appetite for sport

Mr. Williamson, my chief entrusted me with this warrant, pledging me to secrecy and imposing pains and penalties in the event of anything untoward happening   At that time I was not aware of the reason or the necessity for all this secrecy, but I had good cause to be gratified with the confidence which the superintendent placed in me

As the man we wanted was a big, powerful fellow, and a fight might come off, or an attempted rescue be tried, assistance was necessary. I secured, therefore, the aid of a trusty colleague.

The warrant was handed to me in the afternoon, and I immediately made for the neighbourhood where the man lived, and also searched his haunts, but without success. Early next morning—it was a Sunday—we renewed the watching.

It was a dreadfully tedious day; but about seven p m. our man left his house with two of his "pals." It was then quite dark, and the three men walked at a quick pace. We had to make after them at a lively rate, and, hearing us in pursuit, the trio turned into a very dark road and quickened their speed, improving their lead.

Owing to the darkness we were not absolutely sure of our man, but we recognized his form and build

"Now then, run," presently cried one of the men with him.

At this signal off started our man, and I ran after him; but I was suddenly seized round the body by a big fellow—the man who had given the warning—and he put his foot behind me to give me a nasty fall; but I slipped over his foot and freed myself with a great effort from his grasp.

I held in my hand a heavy blackthorn, and without waiting I brought it down heavily upon his head The blow caught the brim of his hat and sent it flying like a shuttle-cock, and its owner reeled on one side and I dashed ahead

Away my colleague and I pelted after the other men, who had profited by these few moments' delay, and in a chase of a few hundred yards we overtook the man for whose arrest I held a warrant

He turned at bay, and his right hand moved towards his hip pocket for his revolver, which he whipped out.

I seized the weapon and shouted, "For Heaven's sake, don't make a fool of yourself, it means murder!"

"I won't," said he, and released his hold of the revolver.

His friends came up, but made no attempt at a rescue, and with the assistance of some constables we put our prisoner into a cab. I took the ruffian who had assaulted me also into custody, but, thinking that our man in the cab was sufficient responsibility, I let the other fellow go, for he pleaded very hard for his liberty and apologized for the obstruction he had caused.

On the following day, while giving my evidence at

Marlborough Street Police Court, four men having now been arrested, I referred to the incident of the assault upon me by the man who was then sitting in the court He was directed to stand up for identification, and was then ordered into custody.

I obeyed the magistrate, arrested the man, and when I was about to search my prisoner I saw him endeavour to destroy some paper.

I struggled with him, and we had a fight for it At length I took the paper from him, much torn.

On putting pieces together I discovered the paper to bear a nicely drawn plan of the cells attached to the court A dotted line ran from the court towards these cells, and then led up some steps and through the police station to a spot marked, against which were the words, "Your trap."

There was another mark designating the place where the gaoler was to be knocked down whilst taking our man from the court to the cells. This prisoner was then to follow the dotted route through the police station in Marlborough Mews to his trap, which would be in waiting.

It appeared that the plan had been drawn from observations made by its author during a visit paid to his friend that morning in the cells, and his object in attending the magisterial investigation was evidently secretly to pass this plan to the prisoner as he left the dock.

Of the ultimate and highly momentous results of the arrests made in connection with the great Turf Frauds it is not necessary for me here to speak.

CHAPTER VI.

THE RUSSIAN GOLD-DUST SWINDLE—A VICTIM TELLS A
STRANGE STORY.

THERE are many cleverly executed frauds and other crimes which come under the notice of the detective in regard to which no arrest may take place, and these matters seldom become public. So many people were victimized by the Russian Gold-Dust Swindle that I am tempted to tell their history.

Not a great while ago a gentleman came to me at Scotland Yard, upon the introduction of a friend, and told me the following extraordinary story

"About two months ago," this gentleman said, "I received a letter from Riga, from a person signing himself 'Posmansky.' I do not know any one in Riga, and the writer was a stranger to me."

"Pardon me," said I, "do you advertise at all?"

"Yes, in a Continental time-table"

"Ah! that would explain it."

My visitor seemed surprised, and exclaimed—

"You seem to know something of this matter already?"

"Pray continue," I said. "You are right—I know a good deal of the story which you are about to tell, but let

me have it in your own way. There has always been a
part of the chain missing, and you may be able to supply
the link that is wanting"

"Well," continued my visitor, "this man Posmansky
wrote to me that he was in search of a gentleman in London
of substantial position and unimpeachable honesty. He
was good enough to say that he had heard of my name
abroad, during his travels, and he very much desired to lay
a business matter before me. It would, he said, require a
comparatively small outlay of capital, but it would return
such a great profit that nothing could prevent my becoming
rich in a very short while. At the same time, though so
profitable to me, it would be sufficiently remunerative to
him to answer his purpose. If I should be willing to enter
into negotiations he would write again and tell me the
nature of the undertaking"

"Of course such a mysterious communication whetted
your curiosity?"

"Certainly it did In that spirit I wrote to Posmansky
for further information"

"That was what Posmansky was playing for," said I.

"I suppose it was. It is all very well to be wise after
the event," answered my visitor ruefully , "at all events, in
a post or two I received another letter from Riga. As
nearly as I can recollect, it stated that Posmansky (the
writer) had a friend—a Jew—who travelled in Siberia, and
sold goods to the gold-miners, and, as was common in
Russia, he combined with his business as a merchant that
of a money-lender, or he accepted things in exchange for
his merchandise for which he could find a market elsewhere.

"This business took him into very isolated places, and to penetrate so far he was required to hold a pass from the Government, for those settlements were inhabited only by political prisoners, who had been exiled to the mines of Siberia. The only free men in such remote spots were the officers having the charge of the prisoners, and, therefore, only a man who was thoroughly trusted—such as this Jew, for example—could be permitted to go amongst these communities

' 'Now,' continued my correspondent, 'these officers who have the care of the prisoners are very poorly paid, and they lead very dull and monotonous lives. To relieve the tedium of existence they gamble extensively, and drink to such an extent that their pay is wholly insufficient for their expenses To make up the deficiency they secrete from time to time gold dust, which they sell to my friend—the Jew merchant—who brings it, at great personal risk, to Riga. But, unfortunately for him, the Russian law forbids any private individual and subject of the Czar to dispose of gold dust. For some time a purchaser who lived in Paris was accustomed to come to Riga and secretly buy the gold dust which had accumulated in the hands of the Jew, but, unfortunately, this buyer has just died, and a fresh purchaser is required.'"

"I have heard this much of the tale before, with variations," I interposed. "Of course the writer suggested that you should become the purchaser?"

"Yes; that was so. The writer said that he and the Jew preferred if possible to find a buyer in London, where the facilities for the sale of gold were unexampled. The correspondent added some figures and calculations, from which it appeared that I should make an estimated profit of two hundred per cent. upon the transaction."

"Without risk?"

'There was no risk, the writer said. All that I should have to do would be to go to Riga put up at a certain hotel, and Posmansky's agent would there call upon me and bring with him the gold dust I was to be permitted to take a sample, which should be melted in my presence, and then forwarded to London to be assayed Supposing that I received a satisfactory report the purchase of the bulk could then and there be completed"

"How much gold dust did Posmansky propose to sell upon this occasion to you?"

"About three hundred pounds' worth, and he said that at the price which it could be sold in London the purchaser would make six hundred pounds profit It was explained that the Jew merchant could afford to part with the gold dust at this low price as he had not given the officers in Siberia very much money for it"

"Did the story tempt you?" I asked.

"Well, it looked a very feasible one, and the bait was not a bad one I must confess this prospect of easily acquired wealth began to grow upon me and dazzle my mind, but for some time I took no further notice of it. I then received another letter from Riga"

"And what had they to say to you in that letter?"

"It was a note simply to ask whether I intended to go to Riga or not. If I did not wish to proceed further they would have to seek some other purchaser There was risk in keeping the gold dust on hand, and the Jew merchant was about to proceed upon another journey to Siberia.

" This letter determined me. I wrote, in reply, stating that I would leave London on the following Thursday, and on my arrival at Riga would repair to the hotel which Posmansky had named.

" Accordingly I went to Riga, and took the precaution of asking a friend, who knew all about the quality of gold, to accompany me He was in the jewellery trade, and knew exactly where the dust could be sold to advantage In fact, he was quite as eager in the matter as I

" My friend considered the affair a piece of good business

' I had been directed in the letter to remain at the hotel until some one should call upon me, as, for reasons which may be understood, it was thought wisest to carry out the transaction in the private room of the hotel

" We waited, but nobody came to see me, and no communication reached us

" ' Has a hoax been played upon me?' I asked my friend.

" ' We shall see,' he said.

" Whilst we were staying at the hotel two men called upon my friend and me. They wished us to purchase cheap jewellery and articles of that kind. I know now why they should have troubled us at all."

" Why?" I asked, having my own views on the matter.

" Simply to make it appear that it is the custom in Riga to wait upon foreign visitors in this way. That was to disarm our suspicions, if we had any; but there was another reason. They came as spies."

" I think you are right"

" Yes, as spies to see what we were like—generally to take stock of us, to form their own ideas as to whether they might safely proceed with the swindle. I believe these two men to have been confederates of the gang. In fact, afterwards I saw one of them watching the hotel, and it is quite clear to me now that we were watched the whole time we were there. You see, they may have thought that whilst they proposed to trick us we were tricking them."

"You mean by giving information to the police?" I said.

"Precisely," returned my visitor. "They watched us to make sure that we did not go to the police, and that the police did not come to us."

"They had a double reason for not desiring that the police should hear of the affair," I suggested.

"I quite understand you. I must candidly confess it never occurred to me at that time that I was running the risk of arrest on the charge of buying gold dust from men who were forbidden by the law to sell it. It was a trap—a cleverly laid one—you see, a trap which was an open door to Siberia, possibly. But let me get on with my story.

"When no one representing Posmansky appeared we began to grow very impatient, and I had some thoughts of returning to England. I had given the Poste Restante as my address, and it was no use to make inquiry for letters there.

"On the evening of the third day, by which time, I suppose, Posmansky believed the coast to be clear, a Russian asked for me.

"It was at dusk, between the lights, and the hour had been purposely selected, no doubt

"My visitor brought with him a heavy bag—one of

leather. He did not explain his mission until by precise inquiries he had satisfied himself that we had really been in correspondence with Posmansky, and, on our part, we took equal precautions to be certain as to the claim of this emissary to address us on the business in hand.

"These preliminaries having been satisfactorily settled, the Russian, in tolerable English, gave a verbal account of the manner in which the gold dust was obtained below its value, and then I asked—

"'Is the dust in that bag?'

"'Yes,' said he, and opening his leather bag he took from out of it another smaller one, made of canvas. This he placed on the table, opened the neck, and displayed its yellow contents in a perfectly frank and open manner There was no concealment whatever

"'I shall require to be satisfied that this dust is gold,' I said

"'Certainly, sir, I have the apparatus here,' and so saying he produced some piping from the leather bag One end of it he adjusted to one of the gas-burners in the room. It diminished the light somewhat.

"Next the Russian took a blow-pipe, and then he dipped his hand into the canvas bag and took out a small portion of dust, which he placed upon a sheet of paper. This sample he handed to us for our inspection.

"My friend scrutinized the dust minutely and carefully.

"'Yes,' said he, 'it *is* gold, right enough.'

"Of course I felt satisfied with his assurance.

"'But I shall melt it and you will see,' said the Russian.

"He took the dust and with his blow-pipe in the gas flame he proceeded to fuse the gold. There was a tumbler of water on the table, and as the metal melted it dropped into the water to cool. When it was cold the Russian took the little lump out and handed it to us for our inspection and test

"My frie tested it, with perfectly satisfactory results, but we were satisfied with this.

"'May we have another sample?' I asked the Russian.

"'Oh yes,' he replied, and stretched out his hand to take it from the bag.

"But my friend was too quick for him

"'Stay,' said he, 'let me;' and in an instant he had dipped his hand into the bag and said to the Russian · 'There, will you melt that?'

"The Russian smiled but said nothing. However, he went through the same business as before. The dust was melted, and the lump of solid gold was given to us in order that it might be forwarded to London for assay.

"Then the bag containing the rest of the dust was securely fastened up and we each affixed our seal to it. The Russian gave me an address which would find him when an answer as to the quality of the gold should reach us from London. Putting his apparatus and the gold dust into his leather bag, the man went away with studied courtesy.

"In due course we despatched the sample to London for assay, and we waited in Riga for a few days pending the reply.

"It came—an official analysis, stating that the gold was twenty-two carat fine.

"'Eureka!' cried my companion.

"We communicated with the Russian. There was a

little delay, but he eventually came to the hotel again, about the same time of the evening as before—that is, when it was neither light nor dark

"I told the Russian that the report from London was quite satisfactory.

"'C'est bien!' said he in French, and forthwith produced the bag which contained the remainder of the gold dust

"My friend scrutinized the seals carefully   They were intact. We had used our own private seals and the wax impressions exactly corresponded"

"Then you had some idea that another bag might have been substituted?" I inquired of the narrator of the story.

'Yes, you will see we took all necessary precautions I went further   'Have you any objection,' said I to the Russian, 'to take out another sample and to test it?'

"'Oh no,' he answered blandly.

"'It is merely business,' explained my friend.

"'In opening a new transaction, gentlemen, you have the right to be careful. When we know each other more we can dispense with these little formalities. but I assure you they give me no trouble—oh no, none.'

"I bowed.

"The Russian fixed his blow-pipe as before, and whilst the melting was in progress the light in the room was considerably lessened

"Finally another lump of gold was handed to us, and my friend, having tested it, expressed himself perfectly satisfied   We then entered into negotiations as to the price of the gold, and having agreed upon the figure the Russian took out a weighing machine from his bag and ascertained the weight In the result we worked out the sum, and I paid the Russian three hundred and twenty pounds for the dust.

"On the following day, with my friend, I returned to London, having met with no difficulty in taking the gold dust away. We might have been the victims of a police plot, you understand, for incriminating suspected officials; but we were not.

"I was anxious to realize my money, and I handed a portion of the dust I had purchased to my friend the jeweller.

"On the following day he came to me with a pale, affrighted face.

"'Heavens, man!' I exclaimed, 'what is the matter?'

"'We have been had clean,' he gasped

"I sank into my chair with far from agreeable sensations

"'The gold dust we brought from Riga,' he continued, 'is nothing but brass—brass filings.'

"And that is what the gold dust really was—brass doctored to resemble gold so closely that even an expert was deceived"

"But the analysts were not wrong?" I hinted to my visitor, as he concluded his tale.

"Oh no," he replied, "the samples that were tested were of pure gold, right enough It was only the bulk which was brass I sold the lot for seventeen shillings"

I have dwelt somewhat in detail upon this narration of facts, concealing or withholding nothing, for it has come to my knowledge that many people in this country have fallen victims to the Russian Gold Dust Swindle. It may be asked how the trick was really done.

"I cannot conceive how they did it," said my visitor "I was watching the Russian the whole time very closely."

"Well," I told him, "don't you see, the man chose a time when the light was bad, and he then simply indulged in the ordinary sleight-of-hand trick, substituting real gold for brass filings at the moment you were called upon to examine the sample."

"And what am I to do now?" my speculating visitor demanded.

"Grin and bear it," I replied. "It won't do for you to show yourself in Russia to tell the authorities that you went over to Riga to buy gold dust, in defiance of the Russian law. Besides I question whether a warrant would be granted here on the information contained in these letters, for the transaction was completed in Russia, out of our jurisdiction."

As I reflect upon this fraud, which is certainly a most ingenious one, the axiom of Bulwer Lytton occurs to me "Every man who seeks a bargain is either a rogue or a fool."

CHAPTER VII.

MY PET CRIMINAL—SOME LEAVES FROM A MISSPENT LIFE.

IT is a very common thing for a detective officer to have a pet criminal, and it is not unusual also for an officer to bestow more attention upon one class of crime than another. At one time my particular bent was the detection of swindling, and my pet criminal was "Bill the Loaner," otherwise known to the world as William Hanbury. Whenever a loan-office swindle was to the front, poor Bill was sure to get the blame.

Bill often came under my notice, and, as we frequently were travelling companions, we called each other by our Christian names. He had been well brought up and educated, could speak French and Italian, and was a well-read man, so the journeys which we took together to Ireland or to Scotland after each arrest were whiled away very pleasantly

Why these loan-office swindlers preferred to operate upon the susceptible, but, as a rule, impecunious Irishman, and his cousin, "the canny Scot," I never could tell.

Perhaps it was because they had formed the opinion that there were more needy people in Ireland and Scotland anxious to borrow money at any cost than anywhere else.

Or they may have imagined that persons who had been defrauded in remote districts would be less likely to enter upon a prosecution But whatever the reason, the gang certainly advertised more freely in the sister countries than in England, and they made many victims in the Green Isle and in the Land of Cakes. Hence our prisoners were invariably charged in Dublin, Belfast, or other Irish towns, or in some Scottish city or burgh.

On one occasion whilst under arrest Hanbury narrated to me the story of how he came to embark upon a career of crime.

"My parents," he said, "were well-to do, and my father held a position of trust, but he died, unfortunately, when I was quite young, and my widowed mother petted me greatly. When I left school I looked out for a clerkship, and answered an advertisement of a certain Dr. W——, of Belgravia, who offered a small salary Dr W—— was the proprietor of a much-advertised cure for deafness, and his correspondence was so large as to employ several clerks in opening the letters to take out the remittances, and forward bottles of the specific in return.

"At that time I was perfectly innocent, but I soon learned that the doctor was a humbug and a quack, his business a swindle, and the clerks a set of thieves. They were accustomed to help themselves to postage-stamps and post-office orders, and I resisted the temptation as long as I could; but one day the doctor detected a robbery of the kind, and gave the delinquent a mild wigging only. I could withstand it no longer, and stole as the others did

"The pilferings went on, and I prospered. First I went to attend patients as an assistant, and afterwards as the principal operator. The bungling over and unskilful handling of some well-to-do people (one noble lord having been nearly killed by the doctor), and complaints insinuating fraud, having reached Scotland Yard, the doings of Dr. W—— occupied the attention of the police, and he was arrested and convicted.

"I was cut adrift. My employer being in prison, my own character was besmirched, and, moreover, I had lost the taste for continuous and honest employment. In such straits, I met a fellow-clerk, who, previously to joining the doctor's staff, had been concerned in loan-office swindling, and I was invited to join a gang of rogues who were engaged in this business.

"As I was a good penman, I soon became the scribe of the gang, and ultimately their chief

"Not long after I took up loan-office swindling a brilliant idea occurred to an old hand, who was undergoing a short term of imprisonment for stealing blankets In the prison library he had found Dickens's 'Martin Chuzzlewit,' and had been much interested in the doings of Montagu Tigg in connection with the Anglo-Bengalee Disinterested Loan and Life Assurance Company, and, reflecting upon what he had read, one morning, while picking oakum, he exclaimed, ' I've got it,' forgetting that the prison rules forbade talking, to which the warder, much astonished, cried, 'Yes, you will get it, if you don't shut up.'

"When this man was released he met his old chums at a special meeting convened at a low public-house in Shoreditch, and he placed his scheme before us, for I was one of the party It was my duty to 'lick it into shape,' and the result was so successful that it had not long been started before we were netting £20 apiece every week."

Now, as I am about to relate how it fell to my lot to capture my pet criminal, in consequence of this scheme, I ought to explain how the loan-office gang worked.

One of their number arranged, on some plausible story, for letters to be received for him at an "accommodation address"—generally a small shop   Then advertisements were inserted in the provincial, Scottish, and Irish newspapers, offering money to lend on note of hand, interest 6 per cent, and, at first, no inquiry fees   Letters in reply poured in, and they were fetched away every morning, directly after delivery, by the "runner," who incurred more risk of arrest than the principal, but who well knew he was scarcely worth the trouble of prosecuting.

He was, however, protected by a confederate or "middleman," who watched the shop every morning before the runner entered it, and gave the signal for him to fetch the letters, if the coast appeared clear. The middleman followed the first man to receive the letters at some convenient spot, in order that they might be taken by him to the principal, who did the office work.

The man who watched the runner also cashed the post-office orders. Thus the work was equally divided between the three, and the risk of detection reduced to a minimum.

I have no space to set forth the correspondence which passed between the loan-office swindlers and their victims —although it is very amusing—for I wish now to relate how I effected Bill's arrest.

When I first made the detection of loan-office swindlers a specialty, their game was being practised to such an extent that the complaints which reached the police were sufficiently numerous to be serious. Everything had favoured the rogues, and they had carried on their operations, first in one part of the metropolis, and then in another, so that no one officer was able to acquire a knowledge of their system of working The local detective was generally asked to make inquiry, and by the t me he appeared upon the scene the swindlers had decamped to another address in a different police division, and the inquiry ended in nothing being done.

For this reason, and in order to suppress the frauds, it was ordered that every complaint should forthwith be taken in hand by the central staff at Scotland Yard, and it became my duty to give particular attention to the work

I studied the matter, and by inquiry soon satisfied myself that the new form of roguery had not been devised by new men altogether, but nad been adopted by old hands, closely allied with the long-firm "school," or gang Loan-office swindling was a fresh idea of theirs—that was all.

Now, at that period, I had a good knowledge of long-firm men, and was able to go among them and get information, and it was in this way that I first discovered that the King of the Loaners was Bill Hanbury

I had a description of this man, but there the information ended ; for Bill was very careful not to permit even his most intimate chums to know his address, and, on their part, they were not disposed to reveal his lurking-place, because their means of livelihood depended to a great extent upon his immunity from arrest. He was the head-piece of the gang

There was a difficulty in finding the man in the first instance, but that was not the chief obstacle, though for a while I did not even know for whom to look, and it was only by piecing together scraps of information that we got upon the track.

The "runner" was, however, "spotted," *i.e.* traced to the "middleman," and the "middleman," by dint of patient observation, to my friend " Bill "—the boss

Sometimes, whilst this "shadowing" was in progress, it would be late at night when Bill was "picked up," that is to say, encountered. I often said to the colleague with whom I worked—

"Well, we are sure of him to-night, as he has taken too much to drink."

But it was precisely on these occasions that instead of going home he would spend the night with one of his " pals," or even would put up at an hotel, by which means our watching went for naught

Surely, although slowly—for all this "shadowing" meant a vast expenditure of time—we traced Bill to a particular locality, and hence came to the conclusion that he must live within a certain circle

We were then enabled to dispense with waiting for the " middleman " to meet Bill in order to give him the letters, for we could make sure of finding Hanbury within a certain area. We took up our position near to this spot and gradually drew the circle closer, so that street by street we followed our man nearer to his home.

But then came a block

Now, it was absolutely necessary that we should find Bill's address, for we hoped to discover at his lodgings evidence which would prove that his handwriting was identical with that of the letters which had been addressed to defrauded clients

My man, however, grew very suspicious, especially when he carried incriminating letters about with him His eyes would be all over the place, and he would dart into dark entries, and sometimes make use of a *cul de sac*, and wait round corners to satisfy himself that no one was on his track.

Then we contrived a ruse.

One morning Bill suddenly turned upon a boy who was at his heels, spinning his top as he went, and he boxed the lad's ears without more ado, saying, "Take that to the 'tec who employed you."

The boy went away bellowing, as had been previously arranged, for Bill was on the right scent—the lad had been in our service for some time—but the little chap's crying so distracted the swindler that he didn't notice another of our spies—a man who was delivering circulars from door to door and .... the side of the street until he ..... able to follow Bill round the corner and note the house which he entered

Then the bill deliverer rejoined my colleague and myself at an agreed upon rendezvous

We sent to the nearest police-station for the assistance of constables should any fighting be on hand

Then we concocted a telegram, which we despatched from a convenient post-office, to Bill "reply paid." This was the way in which we obtained admission to the house, for when the telegram boy delivered his message we stepped into the passage

We caught Bill splendidly, in the very act of writing for inquiry fees and interest in advance for the National Monetary Exchange.

This was William's first arrest. He was taken to Scotland, where the prosecutor lived, and was there convicted and sentenced.

Now, as it happened, the prison fare in Scotland is not very palatable to the hardest mouth and strongest stomach, and I was, some time later, very much amused to hear from the Procurator Fiscal the following story.

Bill, it appeared, when in gaol, in order to be put upon better diet, feigned sickness, but, unfortunately for Bill, the doctor was an Irishman, of the class who habitually mortgage their income and he had actually been one of Bill's victims in the loan-office swindle.

The doctor was quite willing to pass Bill into the infirmary, and even displayed a great anxiety to get him under his care, but he saw clearly that it was a case of malingering, and instead of putting his patient upon more appetizing fare he gave poor William such a taste of medical ingenuity, in contriving exquisite torture without causing real harm, that my pet criminal was soon very glad to discover himself perfectly well again.

I think the doctor felt a little bit hurt that he, a tolerably sharp fellow, should have been swindled like the rest.

Bill himself, when he realized some time afterwards the nature of the doctor's revenge upon him, laughed as heartily as any one.

He had many amusing anecdotes to tell of the way in which he had swindled governors of gaols and even chiefs of police—for all were fish that came to his net.

Bill, at a subsequent period, again fell into the clutches of the law, and I was charged with his arrest. To effect it the difficulties were even greater than in the first instance, but that, as Rudyard Kipling says, is "another story."

Poor Bill Hanbury! he has been again and again convicted for imagining himself possessed of vast wealth which he was ready to lend on terms little short of philanthropic, but such is human nature that I do not believe he would have stooped to petty larceny, and I am sure that he regarded the common thief and the burglar as enemies to society.

He is not singular in this, for a man who becomes proficient in one branch of crime rarely forsakes it for another, and he looks upon his ' profession ' as perfectly legitimate.

During one of his spells of "trying to run straight," Bill did me a good turn.

I met him in a boxing saloon in Shoreditch, to which I had taken some American friends and a dear old New York colleague.

By the side of my pet criminal sat an old "magsman" (thief), who was a little too far gone in drink, which I had not observed. Some time before I had behaved kindly, even generously, to this "magsman," a fact which he had more than once acknowledged, and he had ever afterwards been very civil to me.

The truth is, I had taken him into custody for a ''confidence trick" job, and although I was morally certain he was the right man, the manner of identifying by the prosecutor did not satisfy me, and I allowed my prisoner to go.

But, in the boxing saloon, he was inclined to be very quarrelsome, and whilst talking to Bill I cracked a little joke with him, which he took in a cross-grained way and indulged in strong threats towards me

However, Bill took up the cudgels in my behalf, and turned upon his companion such a look of menace with a significant movement of his fists—which Bill could use pretty well—and expressed himself to such purpose and in language so unmistakable that the brute wavered and I suspect what might have proved a bad quarter of an hour, considering the class of company that filled the saloon

I quote this incident as an illustration of what service an old prisoner will render to an officer who has treated him fairly and kindly.

The last time I saw Bill was when he was standing in the dock of the Old Bailey He made a sign to me that he wished to speak to me. I went to him and he whispered, "Try and get it put in as light as you can for me. I am not so young as I was, and my health has not been very good for some time."

I knew there was no chance of a light sentence if he was convicted.

When the jury were directed to consider their verdict I looked at Bill

He had turned towards the jury box, and on his face there was, oh, such a look of longing appeal to the twelve who were to decide his fate !

And as Bill retreated from the dock, crushed under the weight of the verdict of " guilty," and his sentence to a long term of imprisonment with hard labour, I could not help reflecting what a wasted life his had been, and how much of evil he owed to his first introduction to the advertising doctor.

CHAPTER VIII.

HOW I HAVE USED DISGUISES—"MAKES UP" THAT
ARE NOT OFTEN SUSPECTED.

SOME of my colleagues at Scotland Yard ha . disapproved of disguise, but in my earlier experience
I found it consequently answer my purpose that I still
adhere to the belief that, if judiciously carried out, a
"make-up" is most valuable to the detective, especially in
his younger days.

I do not allude to the ' make-up" which belongs to the
detective of the stage, whose portraiture is no more true to
life than is the caricature which the French actor usually
presents of John Bull. False moustaches and whiskers—at
all events in daylight—are useless aids, but let a detective
put on, I will say, a butcher's smock, apron, and steel and
who would recognize him in his get-up?

I have known a police officer make a very good sweep.
The garb of a curate is frequently used, for it is very easy
to adopt, and disarms suspicion

Once I pretended to be a surveyor commissioned by
the landlord to make plans for repairs, and in this guise
was able to acquire valuable information concerning the
interior of a certain suspected house. I have also played

the part of a sani inspector, with a similar object in view.

On one occasion I made up as a cabman, with an old long coat, and a horse-cloth on my arm, carrying a whip and a badge well displayed.

I had to tell a bogus tale about a fare whom I had set down at the house, and it was only in this way that I could have obtained the information that I required without causing alarm, and perhaps the consequent flight of my man, thus spoiling a month's hard work in one minute.

I walked into the police-station whilst still in my cab-man's "get-up," and, addressing myself to the inspector on duty, who knew me well, I said—

"I have come for my licence."

"What licence?" he asked. "What name?"

"William Smith," I replied.

"I can't find anything about your licence," the inspector cried, after turning over the books. "Who told you to come here?"

"The gentleman who was here last night."

And then I started to laugh, and the inspector shouted—

"Why, it's Mr Littlechild!"

Such "makes-up," or by changing the natural hair upon one's face, can be usefully adopted, and it is foolish for people to say that these disguises are easily penetrable. I recollect an incident of the kind—although it does not come within my professional experiences—which gave me a great deal of confidence in making up.

A friendly licensed victualler bet me a new hat that I could not take him in by wearing a disguise, and I accepted the wager I selected a night when I had been engaged at a concert of the Metropolitan Police Minstrels, of which I was then the leading tenor, and of which troupe, I am proud to say, I was one of the founders, for it exists for the purpose of giving concerts in the various divisions for the benefit of the Orphanage and other police charities, and has for many years past raised in this way an income of over £1000 a year

Whilst still "in the black," and having borrowed a banjo and a "property" hat, I paid my friend a visit. I was at once ordered off the premises when I began my strumming, and, putting my head in the bar, said, in a gruff voice, "Good evening!" and when I ordered a drink I was forcibly ejected by the landlord's barman, who never perceived the trick

Next day I got a solicitor—a friend—to send a lawyer's letter claiming damages for assault, and the landlord, amazed, replied that there must be a mistake, as Mr Littlechild was a great friend of his, and he had not seen him for some days.

On the following evening I again went to the house, with a white face, and, putting my head inside the bar as before, shouted "Good evening!" when the landlord saw through the joke and I won my hat

However, the Experience which I have now to set down had far graver issues

It concerns the arrest of a man whom I have previously described as "my pet criminal"—otherwise "Bill the Loaner"—the prime mover in all loan-office swindles for many years.

Bill was supposed to be living in a densely populated neighbourhood, full of narrow streets, courts, and alleys, which would make the work of "shadowing" his movements far more difficult than what he received in a genteel suburb.

I have already explained that in swindles of this kind our first business was to watch the newspaper shop where letters in answer to loan advertisements were received, then to follow the runner who collected these replies, and so discover the "middleman" to whom he would hand them, and by following the middleman to find the scribe, the head of the gang—that is, Bill himself.

We had succeeded in tracing the letter carrier to the "middleman," and the middleman to an appointment with Bill, but we could not discover where the latter actually lived, although we had formed a pretty shrewd idea as to the neighbourhood. Still, we were at a loss to know the exact street and number

An amusing incident occurred one morning in connection with one of the "runners."

The newsvendor's shop at which the letters were received had a back entrance, which was unknown to the conspirators. I arranged with the newsagent to allow me to take up my position at the back of the shop very early, having entered the premises by the back door

From this point of vantage I could see right into the street, and I then observed that a confederate of the gang was on the watch. I noticed him give a signal which clearly meant "All right," and then disappear.

In a few moments a man came into the shop and asked for "Mr. Baring's" letters. They usually selected the name of some well-known banker or City magnate in which to advertise

The letters were given to him and away he went, and I did not know at the time, but I was afterwards informed, that he was the son of an old loan-office swindler.

He stepped out briskly, and as I had to leave the shop by the back way he was some distance ahead when I picked him up

After following him for some distance it occurred to me that some signal had been conveyed to the young fellow, for his gait betrayed a certain indecision and nervousness He didn't seem to know which way to turn. Afterwards I recollected that I had seen a man lounging against an iron post at the corner of the street, and although I saw him give no positive sign to the "runner," such a warning must have been conveyed by him to the man who carried the letters.

However, afterwards I had no doubt that this lounger was the "middleman" to whom the letters should have been handed by the "runner."

The ' runner" whom I was "shadowing" walked aimlessly up and down one or two streets, not daring, apparently, to look behind him; but at length, in sheer desperation, he did glance round, and as I was less careful at that stage about my "shadowing," seeing that my man knew that he was under observation, as he turned our eyes met

I shall never forget the scared look which passed over his face.

Yet I have seen many scared faces in my time. The effect of fright produced by a totally unexpected arrest is very varied in its nature, let me say in passing. I recollect one person, who looked perfectly cool a moment before,

suddenly throw off a vapour like steam, completely envelop-
ing him in a cloud, which was the strangest thing I have
ever witnessed.

On this occasion the man, with the instinct of self-
preservation, threw down his letters and took to his heels,
and as he was a long, lanky fellow, with no spare flesh, he
succeeded in covering the ground rapidly

It was a second race of Atalanta I stooped to pick up
the letters, and gave my man such a good start that,
although I feigned a pursuit, I saw that the chase was
hopeless, and I have not seen him since

I learned afterwards that although the young fellow was
perfectly well aware that he had thrown me off, he never
ceased running until he reached St. George's Barracks,
where he enlisted in a regiment for service abroad His
friends all thought he was arrested and taken to Ireland,
until they received a letter from India, where the lanky
" ner" was on the road to promotion in a lancer
regiment

Bill, later, told me that on the return to England of his
old companion he paid him a visit, and found him look
exceedingly smart in his uniform. He asked him if he was
not going to pay his respects to Mr Littlechild.

' No, thank you," replied the long soldier "I have
seen him once, and that is quite enough for me '

To return to Bill and his second arrest, we remained in
ignorance as to his lurking-place. I was informed, however, that he was now the consort of a woman neither fair
fat, nor forty, but something between each. They were
making a living in a questionable way, but which was not
subject to the criminal law.

Now, this lady, I gleaned, had strong economical views ; and in the second place she kept a pet dog—a cross between a poodle and Maltese—which accompanied her wherever she went.

These two points furnished me with my clue.

I immediately turned my attention to the facilities for cheap marketing in the neighbourhood where, as I suspected Bill was living. One particular street was given up to costermongers, and I resolved to haunt it regularly at such times as such a careful housewife as Bill's would make her purchases at the stalls.

"It will never do," I reflected, "to knock about this locality in West-End-made clothes."

So I "made-up" by selecting from my wardrobe a skull-cap and spotted scarf, to be tightly tied round the neck, and the other essentials of a Whitechapel rig-out. My face I left unshaven for a day or two, and in such natural disguise—which you will see does not at all correspond with the theatrical ideas current upon the subject—I began to frequent the street market.

My object was to discover a dog of a mixed poodle and Maltese breed.

But the place seemed infested with long-haired dogs of mixed descent, and in each case I "shadowed" their owners to their houses without success.

Everything comes to the man who knows how to wait and the waiting is a thing to which a detective must accustom himself. and on the fourth day I was rewarded.

I "spotted" the dog, and also the woman who owned the animal. Further, I was able to follow them to her home, which was in a very short cross-street connecting two parallel streets—in fact, a position which made an arrest a very awkward job to effect

Yet an arrest—at a time when there was a probability also of securing documents in the prisoner's possession necessary to the prosecution—was essential to a conviction It was obvious that such a capture could only be made by a *coup*.

On the following morning I reconnoitred the spot right early.

Nothing attracted my attention until 7 30 a m , when the milkman went down the street and past Bill's house, crying, " Milk O¹" Just before he got to the door it opened, and a girl's head was thrust out

Upon this incident my plans were formed.

Bill, when he liked, could be a dangerous customer, so in making my arrangements for the following morning I thought it well to have two policemen in uniform at hand when the attempt to enter the house was made

A very able colleague assisted me in the case—a good and determined officer, somewhat pugnacious, perhaps, if "rubbed the wrong way," but this is rather a qualification than otherwise. Certainly it was such in his case.

Now, when next morning arrived, we carefully posted our uniform men out of sight, with instructions not to show themselves until we had entered the house

At the hour when the milkman ought to have been in the street—he was late that morning—I set up the familiar call, " Milk O ! milk O !"

The ruse was perfectly successful, and the untidy head of the girl popped from out the doorway of Bill's house. In a moment I had pushed into the hall, and before the girl had recovered from her fright my colleague had followed me.

"Hush!" I said, and we went upstairs to the front room, guessing that this should be the point to make for

"Search the other room," I whispered to my colleague; for there was a possibility that another member of the gang was living with Bill. I entered the front room.

Bill and the woman were in the room. In an instant the man had jumped out and seized me, but I had expected such an attack, and gripped him in such a way that he was powerless.

Hearing the noise of a scuffle my assistant returned, and rapidly taking in the situation, he seized a hair-brush from the dressing-table and threw it with a crash through the window into the street below. It fell, with the broken glass, upon the two policemen in waiting.

This was the signal for them. They came upstairs, and Bill, directly he saw them, promised to be on his good behaviour.

I may say this little episode in no way ruffled my temper, and it did not disturb the friendly relations existing between Bill and myself.

We started as very pleasant travelling companions for Ireland, and on the journey Bill enlightened me upon several points of his career which I have already recorded. In due course he was convicted, and passed in consequence another fair slice of his life within the walls of a gaol.

CHAPTER IX

HOW I DISCOVER CLUES—MYSTERIES AND THEIR UNRAVELLING.

I HAVE been asked, "How do you get your clue; in what way do you fix upon a theory; what leads you to make the first step in a chain of investigation which is to lead to an arrest?"

Two or three experiences that come to my mind illustrate the methods upon which I have sometimes worked, and they will answer the above question.

It happened that a gang of thieves had devised a very good plan for securing booty, by putting forward one of their number to act as a solicitor's clerk. The young fellow selected by his confederates really had been in a lawyer's office. He had been a precocious lad, brought up in one of those institutions which take boys from the gutter and put them into good situations.

I should here like to record that I have nothing to say against charitable agencies of the kind, and it is my experience that the percentage of lads who have been trained in them, and who afterwards "go wrong," is not greater than the proportion of boys who turn out bad, although they may have received their education in our best public schools.

The general desire of "reclaimed" lads is to shake off their old associates; but in the case now before me the young fellow had drifted back into low companionship after having acquired a knowledge of engrossing and copying which stood him in good stead in the paths of crime.

Young Smooth first began his career as a "cracksman" by working "single-handed"—*i.e.* alone. His plan was very simple. He would procure a situation at some distance from London, and behave as an industrious, well-conducted clerk, taking the greatest interest in his work and disarming all suspicion.

He appeared perfectly greedy for work, and when his employers had learned thoroughly to trust him it was the most natural thing for young Smooth to remain busy in the office at night after the other clerks had gone home, or were enjoying themselves.

"Smooth," exclaimed one solicitor, in the hearing of his whole staff, "Smooth is a fine fellow—he is an example to you all, and we shall see him at the head of his profession"

Smooth, however, had a different ambition, and instead of spending his "overtime" in copying deeds, as his employer supposed, he devoted it to the investigation of locks and patent safes, with the view to the removal of as much portable property in the form of postage stamps and petty cash as he could lay hands upon.

Then, with the spoil, he departed one night for London, and in the great metropolis he ran across his old companions and imparted to them the particulars of his mode of earning a livelihood. They fully approved of it, and a gang was formed to carry on the "business" on a more extensive scale.

Smooth obtained another situation, once more played the part of the praiseworthy clerk, was trusted, was left behind in the office at night to clear up arrears, and then, having carefully planned the "job," communicated with his confederates that the "swag" might be expected, and set to work as a safe-breaker, clearing off with the proceeds of the robbery to fresh woods and pastures new, as before.

Of course Smooth, in order to carry a sequence of such burglaries into successful operation, needed to obtain a series of situations, and the more easily to get them he made use of the letter-writing abilities of one of his confederates, who fabricated a number of testimonials. The situations were, in the first instance, heard of by Smooth himself, who regularly advertised or answered advertisements in the law newspapers.

At length, the robberies having become very serious, the matter was entrusted to me, and little by little I learned the particulars which for convenience I have set out in narrative form. But at the outset all that I had to work upon was the fact that the man's name was Smooth, and that he had had several "accommodation addresses"—generally, as I have previously explained, small shops where letters are received at a penny each, to oblige people who have no address of their own, or who wish to keep it secret.

I should add that a specimen of Smooth's handwriting was given to me.

Now, the theory which I resolved to work upon suggested itself suddenly. Sometimes in a perplexing case I have gone home and had my first sleep, and then in the middle of the night have clearly perceived the plan of action before me, when up to that moment the affair had seemed in a hopeless tangle. In this case I had not to wait for an idea.

I went to a friend of mine who was a solicitor.

"Will you allow me to make use of your name and office?" I asked, having explained the circumstances to him.

"Certainly," he replied.

I thereupon wrote out an advertisement stating that the services of a clerk were required by a country lawyer, and application was to be made in the first instance to Mr. X——, solicitor, Bedford Row

"Will you have this inserted in a law newspaper?" I asked my friend, and accordingly it was done.

I need hardly explain that this advertisement was intended as a bait to catch my sharp young gentleman, Mr. Smooth, as it was phrased in pretty nearly the same terms as the advertisements had been which he had answered on previous occasions Further, I calculated that the haul which the gang had made on their last attempt would by this time have been squandered, and that Mr. Smooth would be on the look-out for a fresh opening for the exercise of his genius.

Replies to my advertisement flowed in so numerously that the work of examining them and of ascertaining whether one of them corresponded with Smooth's hand-writing proved to be a very laborious task.

No result followed from the first advertisement, but, confident of my plan, it was repeated, varied slightly.

Then there was a "bite." Mr. Smooth took the bait and wrote under a feigned name for an appointment. At all events, a letter came which I believed to be in his calligraphy.

The course was clear. An appointment was made with Mr. Smooth that he might have a personal interview with his future employer, who would attend at Bedford Row, and he was asked to give references

On the day named I assumed, not for the first time, the part of a legal practitioner, and awaited in the office the coming of my young friend.

At the hour fixed he was ushered in—a pleasant, prepossessing young man of five and twenty.

My friend, the genuine solicitor, was with me.

Now, the danger was that the gang might have sent some one to pass as Mr. Smooth. It was quite possible that they had gained some knowledge of my plans and were attempting to outwit me. Besides, as the London police were acting for a country chief constable, and no witnesses were on the spot to swear to identification, it would have been an awkward business to have arrested a confederate or a dupe instead of the principal. So I had to be very wary in my efforts to satisfy myself that I was not being deceived I had no portrait of Smooth to guide me, and the applicant gave me another name, as I have said.

"Your name," said I to our visitor, " is Mr. Bright?"

" Quite so," said he.

" And you have had some experience of the duties which will fall to you?"

"Oh yes," he answered.

I put to him a number of questions to test his knowledge, as it might seem, and, having made up my mind that Mr. Bright corresponded with the description given of Mr. Smooth, asked him for a specimen of his hand-writing.

"Sit down here," I said, motioning him to a desk, "and let me see how you write."

I had prepared myself with a phrase containing as many as possible of the words which appeared in the specimen of Smooth's handwriting forwarded to me.

"What shall I write?" said he.

Then I dictated this phrase, and, as he wrote it in fair legal hand, I stood behind his chair with a paper crumpled in my fingers unseen by him.

That paper was the specimen of Smooth's handwriting, sent to me by the country police; and as the man wrote I referred casually to it, and noted that, although Smooth disguised his identity by taking another name, he had not thought of disguising his handwriting, for the original and the phrase written under my eyes at my dictation corresponded exactly.

"That will do," I said.

Something in my tone caused the man to turn and look me in the eyes.

"Mr. Smooth," I said, dropping all disguise, "I am Inspector Littlechild of Scotland Yard, and I arrest you on a warrant which I hold in my hand."

Thereupon Mr. Smooth, *alias* Mr. Bright, fainted dead away in downright earnest, and when he "came to" he found himself my prisoner.

I recollect another incident, in connection with which a probable solution of the mystery suggested itself, to my mind, as a reasonable one directly the facts were made known to me.

I had been on duty at Scotland Yard all night in charge of the office, when, about eight o'clock in the morning, a country superintendent of police introduced to me a certain family solicitor, who had accompanied him to town in great haste. They had arrived by the first train from the North, and were in pursuit of two runaways—the heiress to considerable property, who was a ward in Chancery, and her lover.

"Where do you suppose they have gone?" I asked.

"There is every reason to believe," replied the family solicitor, "that they have come to London. Can we have the assistance of an officer to trace them?"

"Certainly; but what do you imagine their plans are?"

"Probably to take a trip to the Continent"

"Well," said I to the superintendent of police, "what do you propose to do?"

"It will be desirable to find, if we can, the cab which must have taken them from Euston yesterday."

"Very good; but has it not occurred to you why they should have come to London?"

"No," he answered.

"Isn't it just probable that the young lady and her admirer have come here to get married?"

The idea appeared never to have struck them before, and they were very ready to take my advice.

So I drew up a plan.

"Obviously," I said, "they cannot get married, except at a registrar's office, by licence. Now, what you have to do is to inquire whether the gentleman has taken the preliminary steps at any registrar's office."

Very speedily I had drawn up for them a list of the offices to which it was probable that a stranger to London might go. When we began to name them they were not very many, and what might have seemed an interminable task became a simple matter.

Each of the party took a district, and a colleague, who was the first to come upon duty that morning, was allotted to one of these districts.

At ten the hunt began, before midday this officer returned with the information that a gentleman, answering to the description given, had made inquiry of a certain registrar not far from Somerset House, and fixed an appointment for the following morning, when the necessary licence would have been procured.

A telegram was immediately sent to the guardian of the young lady, and he arrived in London that night.

Next morning, as I am informed, for I was not present, the whole party repaired to the registrar's office, and, by permission, secreted themselves in cupboards and odd places, there to await the arrival of the expectant couple.

The runaway pair duly came with a friend—a lady—and were about to fulfil the formalities required of them, when, to their surprise and amazement—for they were totally unsuspicious—a sort of unrehearsed copy of Sheridan's screen scene took place.

First to emerge from his place of concealment came the superintendent of police, and at the sight of him the bridegroom-elect fell "all of a heap" into the fireplace amongst the fire-irons.

Then the guardian of the young lady appeared, and she shrieked and her friend fainted.

The family solicitor stalked, like the proverbial skeleton, from the cupboard.

And Smart—the detective from Scotland Yard—with the registrar himself in the background, completed the group.

I am sorry to add that I cannot conclude this story with the customary ending, " And they were married and lived happily ever afterwards," for, although it was an affair of true love, the course of it ran so awkwardly that the law prevented the marriage of the ward in Chancery to the gentleman with whom she had eloped.

In another case, quite of a different character, the facts supplied no shadow of a clue to work upon.

A woman, who was parted from her husband, and lived by herself, was discovered at her own house nearly murdered. She had sustained very serious injuries, inflicted by some unknown hand, but suspicion pointed to her husband, a man answering to his description having been seen in the neighbourhood just before the crime was committed. No weapon of any kind such as might be used to deal the deadly blows upon the woman's head was found.

The inquiry was not put into my hands at the first, and when I took it up, the would-be murderer had had two or three days' start.

I formed a theory, with nothing to base it upon, that the man would probably return to his old haunts. Therefore in searching the premises afresh, I hunted for any scrap of information pointing to the man's previous movements.

Amongst a lot of old letters I found one which implied that the man had formerly belonged to a club at a village in another county.

Acting upon theory, I immediately began to walk in that

direction, not taking, however, the direct road, but choosing by-paths and calling at wayside alehouses and farmhouses to ascertain whether any such person had asked for food or drink.

It was a cold scent at first, but at last I picked up the trail. A man had been seen. Gradually I drew upon him and lessened the distance between us, and after two days' tracking down, I came upon the would-be murderer, who was wandering aimlessly about the country roads, with the bill-hook with which he had nearly killed his wife still in his possession.

CHAPTER X

BETRAYED BY A "COPPER'S NARK"—HOW A BOGUS
BANK SCHEME WAS FRUSTRATED.

A "COPPER'S NARK' brought to me one day information which astounded me

I dislike the use of thieves' slang—Mr. Williamson disapproved of it, and it was seldom used during my time at Scotland Yard—so I adopt the term above quoted with reluctance, but it is one which is very well known to the police, if not to the public.

Nevertheless, an erroneous impression prevails that a "copper's nark" means an informer. A "nark," or "nose," is usually nothing of the sort, although he gives information to the police. An informer—and I speak with some considerable experience of this genus—is a man who himself has been implicated in a crime, and turned "Queen's evidence" for the sake of securing his own safety, and perhaps making sure of his own neck. But a "nark," or informant, is in reality a humble and more or less regular auxiliary of the detective, and as such I have been accustomed to refer to him

I have always been a believer in the judicious employment of the "auxiliary," but never to rely upon him so entirely as detectives did in my early days, when constables were often on duty in "plain clothes." I am very much afraid that these officers were often led by the nose by the "nark," and the methods they adopted in procuring convictions were not such as would be permitted to-day, for they were not above fabricating the missing links in a chain.

There was a class of detective who believed implicitly in the "nark," and even if they did not do so they used him as a tool, for in the early history of the detective police few men possessed the education or intelligence to work out theories based upon logical deduction which characterizes the detective of to-day, who—I must say, by the way—uses less slang than is supposed. Mr. Williamson, who was my chief superintendent for many years, never countenanced slang.

Of course, a detective cannot plead ignorance of thieves' jargon; but he would require to be well versed in it to be an adept in the use of its ever-changing forms, which vary with every class of criminal, and are constantly altering in fashion.

But, although the modern detective seldom says a man has had "three moon for dipping," when he means to intimate that a prisoner has been sentenced to three months for picking pockets; or that he has had "two stretch for a crack"—*i.e.* two years for burglary—the term "nark" is not yet obsolete, nor is this singular profession

I have to confess that the "nark" is very apt to drift into an *agent provocateur* in his anxiety to secure a conviction, and therefore he requires to be carefully watched.

Now, when the "nark" imparted to me the intelligence

which positively amazed me, I reflected that I had employed this individual many times before, and never had had occasion to distrust him.

Yet the enormity of the crime which he told me was contemplated made me cautious, especially as the story had, as he said, come to his hearing second-hand. It related to an entirely new departure in the annals of swindling.

The "nark' happened in the course of his narrative to mention the name of a man I knew to be an "old hand" at roguery; and, as he had just been liberated from prison, having served five years, and was probably anxious to "get to work" again, the revelations made to me interested me greatly.

And this is what the "nark" told me —

"While in prison Jim Gale (as I shall call him) worked side by side with a convict who had been a bank clerk, but who was doing his five years' penal servitude for robbing the bank at which he had been employed. They were frequently together, these two, and by means of agreed-upon signs and signals, and sometimes in open conversation when a word or two was possible, the warder having turned his back, they communicated with each other and struck up an acquaintance.

"In the silence of his cell, and helped by the seclusion of his life in gaol, the bank clerk had hit upon a scheme by which he hoped to net a very large sum of money— some thousands of pounds. Particulars of this scheme he promised to give to his chum; and as the two were released together a little while ago, they arranged to meet each other and go into partnership."

"What is their idea?" I asked, keenly interested

"This," replied the "nark," "and I may tell you the pair did meet as arranged, or I should not be able to tell you their plans. They propose to take offices in the City, furnish them nicely, and open a bogus bank."

"A bogus bank! What for? To swindle their customers?"

"No, that is not the scheme at all. They propose to use it as a cover for negotiating bills, etc. This business would necessitate the calling upon them at intervals of 'walk clerks' from one or more of the leading banks, who would collect bills of them in the usual way.'

"That will take time, and capital too."

"Ah, there's more of them in it than Jimmy Gale, though I haven't been told their names; and some of the gang are resolute fellows."

Of course, in big "jobs" of the kind, there is always some one in the background with money to carry it through, if necessary.

Proceeding with his tale, my auxiliary said—

"When they are ripe for pulling their job off, they propose to so fix up things that a clerk representing a good bank doing a large business shall call upon them.

"Immediately the clerk opens his wallet to withdraw a bill, it is arranged that he shall be seized from behind and dragged into a back room. They are going to gag him and bind him, hold a pistol to his head, and threaten to blow out his brains if he makes the least stir or noise."

"And they then will relieve him of his wallet?"

"Yes, but they don't propose to make a bolt of it straight away. The man who is the ex-bank clerk, and who concocted the scheme, has undertaken to run through the contents of the wallet, separate the cash from the bills waiting collection and drafts which can be presented for payment over the counter, and then complete the round in a cab, which is to be in waiting, making his haul richer at every call. Of course, he knows all about the duties of a walk clerk—that is the kernel of the whole thing."

"And what do they imagine they will make over it?"

"Twelve to fourteen thousand pounds."

The "nark" added that directly the outdoor part of the plot was successfully executed, a messenger was to be sent to the bogus bank, and the gagged man was then to be locked in a safe, to get out of it as best he could, and the rest of the gang were to make their escape

Extraordinary and improbable as this story appeared, the communication was altogether too serious to be ignored, and my chiefs decided that they could not disregard it and run the risk of the plot being carried out.

Observation was ordered to be placed upon Jimmy Gale, with the object of testing the truth of the story, if possible.

Gale's whereabouts were easily ascertained. He had embarked with an old "pal" in the Long Firm line, and had taken imposing-looking offices in the City, carrying on business under a high-sounding name.

We "shadowed" Gale, and in a day or two followed him to a certain restaurant, where he met an individual whom—having the prison photographs at command—we had no difficulty in recognizing as the ex-bank clerk, the alleged author of the iniquitous scheme.

The pair held some earnest conversation, and then made towards the West End.

Now, at this stage, a great surprise awaited me.

Gale I had known for years, and when I first caught sight of his companion I seemed to have some idea that I had seen him before; but I struggled vainly for some time to "fix" him.   At length, however, my recollection suddenly returned, and I recognized the ex-bank clerk as a former "client" of my own—a man of the name of Mortimer, whose arrest I myself had made nearly four years before on a charge of robbing the bank at which he was engaged.

No wonder, however, that I failed to know him at once; for the long term of imprisonment had greatly altered the pale-faced bank clerk, who was now a swarthy, "travel-complexioned" man.

I did not feel so certain that Mortimer would not know me, so I held aloof, for fear that he and Gale might suspect that their plans were known to the police.

It had been reconsidered by my chiefs whether the gang might not be permitted to carry their operations out; but the fear was that a bank clerk—who, of course, could not be let into the secret—would be so greatly terrorized by the gagging, although he might be immediately released by officers on the alert, that his nerves would be permanently injured—even if nothing more serious happened.

Still, I was hoping that something would turn up to cause the conspirators to be as richly punished as they deserved.

It was not difficult to "shadow" Gale and Mortimer as they strolled westwards, so intent were they upon their plotting.   They spent that day in looking over vacant offices in the quarter which it had been indicated to me had been selected by them, and they made, too, all the preliminary inquiries which were necessary prior to taking a set of offices for a term.

Their main object, which next engaged them, appears to have been how to raise the money which would be required.

Had I had the power possessed by the Continental police, I could have laid these rogues by the heels on definite charges of attempted fraud. Their arrest would have at once supplied evidence to make my case. All that the detective wants is justification enough to protect him in taking this initial step; for when the arrest is effected, a letter, a scrap of paper, some article found on the prisoner among his effects, or other trifle, may furnish the police officer with his necessary tools. The counsel call these things "exhibits," but to the detective they are "silent witnesses."

I was in this position when, although I could do nothing with the rascals, as regards the bogus bank scheme, I resolved not to drop the case. I continued my observation, and two days later Gale was seen by me to leave his Long Firm offices, accompanied by his partner. This man, I believe, was not admitted into the bogus bank scheme at all.

Both men carried, however, a number of heavy parcels, and their manner told me distinctly that they had something on foot.

A detective, by careful watching, can learn to read almost the thoughts of the man he has "under observation," and can discover when to relax his vigilance and when to redouble it.

"What is the meaning of this move?" I conjectured.

They went towards Oxford Street, and very soon all speculation on {my part as to their game was at an end, for having reached Holborn they began to relieve themselves of their loads very simply.

Thus, one man would enter a pawnbroker's alone, leaving his "pal" to mind all the parcels but one, which was taken into the shop. The package was pledged, and the two men then proceeded to the next pawnshop. Here the other man took his turn and went inside with another parcel selected from the heap, whilst his confederate remained on guard in the street over the rest. In this way, change and change about, they visited many establishments of the kind until, gradually, they had pawned all their parcels.

Meanwhile I was carefully noting down—unperceived by them—the time, place, and description of each parcel as it was pledged, with a view to future identification.

Having completed this work, Gale and his friend went about enjoying themselves, and I left them to their own devices, quite satisfied with the day's work, feeling sure that I had obtained evidence enough to stop one of the gang, at any rate, from sharing in the plunder of a bank clerk's wallet.

Next day I visited all the pawnbrokers' shops at which the men had called, and obtained, readily enough, a description of the goods put into pawn. In several cases the parcels still bore the name and address of the wholesale houses which had supplied the articles to the Long Firm.

The next step was to call upon the wholesale people who had thus been defrauded. Some of them had been victimized to a considerable extent; for the goods which had been pawned formed a small portion only of those which had been supplied to Gale and his partner.

This partner, I ascertained, had also been convicted on a previous occasion.

Warrants were granted, and very soon both men were arrested, and charged at the police court.

It proved exactly as I had surmised, that if I could only get grounds on which to arrest, no difficulty would arise as to evidence; for among the papers seized, some were found disclosing an extensive system of swindling. I was also able to bring forward evidence in support of the charge that these men had obtained large quantities of goods on fictitious cheques at another address.

The prisoners were sentenced at the Old Bailey. Gale's confederate owed his punishment entirely to his having been with Gale; for if it had not been for the bogus bank scheme in which the latter was engaged, attention might not have been directed to him.

But, as a proof that men do not always get their deserts, Mortimer—the prime mover in the whole affair of the bogus bank—was not arrested, for there was no evidence upon which he could be convicted

A hint was, however, given to him—quite explicit enough for him to understand its meaning; and he must have profited by it, for I have not heard of his having been in any "trouble" since.

CHAPTER XI.

BREAKING UP A SHAM LOAN-OFFICE GANG—WHAT WRITING
A CHEQUE LED TO.

I HAVE had occasion in my Reminiscences to allude
more than once to a class of loan office swindlers who
batten upon victims who are fleeced of inquiry fees, or are
required to pay the interest in advance, but this class of
rogue has to take a back seat when he is put by the side
of the type of man I shall now describe.

Complaints respecting numerous offices which pretended
to make advances of cash to needy people, but which failed
to do so, reached Scotland Yard continually, and the correspondence placed in the hands of the police from time to
time disclosed a new system of doing business.

On the face of it, this business appeared to be perfectly
legitimate. To-day there are many men who are amassing
wealth by purely legal methods, for much of the profit of
loan-office transactions accrues from inquiry fees, and there
is no fraud at all, although, of course, people think themselves aggrieved often enough and make complaints.

It appeared, however, from the papers which were put
into my hands, that a particular firm of civil engineers, who
went by the name of Bruton and Co., Lincoln's Inn Fields,

were advertising pretty extensively in the London as well as leading provincial papers, offering to lend money on note of hand simply, without bill of sale or security. Bruton and Co. duly figured in the Post Office Directory, and to all appearances were of undoubted respectability; but they made no advances.

Inquiry fees were, of course, exacted, and some sort of inquiry did, as a rule, take place, but, whenever possible, the matter ended with a refusal to lend the money asked for, on the ground that the borrower's position was not good enough to warrant the loan. But in other cases the plea put forward was, that before the proposal for the advance could be entertained, the applicant would have to insure his or her life, the policy forming a collateral security.

Further, it was suggested that the policy should be taken out at the Albion Assurance Office in Chancery Lane.

In a great many instances the policy had been duly obtained, nominally for double the amount of the loan, and, in some cases, the premiums paid were over £100 per annum.

After the first premium had been paid, Messrs Bruton and Co. were accustomed to raise the question of a surety, knowing human nature pretty well—for the last thing which an impecunious tradesman will do is to tell somebody else that he is attempting to borrow money.

Having, however, obtained the one surety, the loan-office firm would raise objections to his standing, and the borrower would then be asked for a bill of sale As bills of sale are publicly registered, the fact that a tradesman has given one tends to jeopardize his credit. This circumstance naturally deterred many people from proceeding further, and they had to put up with the loss of their inquiry fees and the premiums paid on the life policy. Fully ninety per cent of the applicants were shaken off in this manner.

Those borrowers who still persisted, having yielded to all demands made upon their faith, were coolly asked, upon printed forms, to go before a magistrate and make such a declaration of solvency as would imply that they did not require a loan at all.

Now, I have thus lightly described this system, because it explains what is to follow, and it shows the safeguards by which Messrs. Bruton and Co. and other firms of the same character surrounded themselves. In the opinion of Scotland Yard at that time no action could be taken by the police, and persons who made complaints were advised to consult a solicitor or to go to a magistrate. We said, further, that if a warrant were granted the police would, of course, execute it.

It is often a trivial matter which starts a very big case. It was so in this instance.

A poor Irishwoman had applied for a loan, had sent the inquiry fees, insured her life, and could not, after all, obtain an advance. She could ill afford the loss, so she came to London, called at the office in Lincoln's Inn Fields, and failing to get redress, made a complaint to Scotland Yard.

I went with her to Bow Street Police Court that she might make a statement to the magistrate. The late Mr. Flowers—a very genial and kind-hearted man—was on the bench, and his powers far exceeded those of the police. He suggested that I should take the woman to the office of Bruton and Co., to ascertain whether the firm would do anything for her.

Now, this suggestion provided an opportunity which we required, for we could not act upon our own initiative.

I accompanied the woman to Lincoln's Inn Fields, and at the offices of Bruton and Co., civil engineers, had an interview with a portly, stately, white-waistcoated gentleman —a man of pleasing manners, with the bump of benevolence largely developed, a greasy, winning smile, an unctuous voice, and a big, flabby hand

"Mr Littlechild," said he, "I have the pleasure of making your acquaintance, and as for this lady, we will see what we can do. Of course, you understand, we are merely agents in this matter for large capitalists—private people, you know. Do you wish to inspect our books?"

I said I did, and accordingly ledgers were produced, kept in apple-pie order, duly balanced, and seemingly perfectly straight. They were placed before me in the most open manner possible.

"You see, Mr. Littlechild, that we are doing a large business"

"It would seem so," I answered, accepting what explanations he offered without demur.

"Of course," the well fed, self-complacent gentleman continued, "it is a pity that there should be so many people in the world wanting money, but we have to take things as they are. Now, if our firm has money to lend, obviously we must take ordinary precautions, lest we should be swindled of it. Do you follow me? Yes, of course. No doubt the majority of these people who apply for loans are honest folk—like this good lady. Quite so. But there are, Mr. Littlechild, and *you* know it as well as anybody" (tapping his snuff-box as he spoke and proffering it to me)—

"there are, my dear sir, a great many rogues in the world Oh yes, sad rogues, and we must protect ourselves against them by inquiries and so forth—at their expense."

"But," said I, "this poor woman is not dishonest, Mr.——"

"Smythe, sir—Nicodemus Smythe. We will admit that this lady is honest. Yes, I will not discuss that; but a great many people begin by being honest, and, under temptation, become—well, yes, otherwise. Do you follow me? But the point for us is, what can we do for this lady?"

"Precisely."

"Well," said he, referring to some papers, "I find that we cannot grant a loan—in justice to our clients we really cannot. But I will make an exception It shall be my own private matter. I will return this lady the inquiry fees"

"And the premium on the life policy?"

"My dear sir, my very dear sir, what have I to do with the life office or its business? You should go to them, sir, for that."

"Very well, then, Mr. Smythe. This lady will be glad of her inquiry fees."

Then Mr. Smythe blundered, for he sat down to his desk and wrote me a cheque, and that cheque was signed "Nicodemus Smythe."

Now, we had much desired to know at what bank Bruton and Co. kept their account, but what struck me as exceedingly strange was this. why should the cheque be signed "Nicodemus Smythe," and not "Bruton and Co."? Why should this gentleman give me a private cheque? For, of course, his excuse that he was going to treat the affair as a private matter was mere talk.

I went with the woman to the bank, and the cheque was duly cashed.

It is not always that bankers will disclose information concerning a customer's account; but in this case we did succeed, on inquiry, in learning of them that Bruton and Co. were not clients of theirs, but the cheques which were given to the firm were paid into Nicodemus Smythe's account.

Further, it appeared that sums were constantly being received in the form of country cheques and post-office orders, but that the outgoings were limited to cheques drawn to meet tradesmen's bills and office expenses. In a word, there were no items to show that the firm, through Mr. Smythe, were advancing sums of money in large or small amounts.

By dint of patient observation I had gathered a good deal of information in the earlier stages of the inquiry concerning the private character of Mr. Nicodemus Smythe. Lincoln's Inn Fields always contains a number of loiterers, waiting outside solicitors' offices, and it was not difficult to stand about unobserved in the morning and in the afternoon to note who were the members of the firm of Messrs. Bruton and Co., and who were the men first to go to the office and the last to leave it.

One night I followed Mr. Smythe westwards. He used to drive to and from his office in a brougham. I traced his carriage to one of the most fashionable streets in Brompton.

Now, it happened that in this particular neighbourhood there was an hotel-keeper who had on several occasions

assisted the police. Naturally, I went to him, and he, by
a stroke of luck, was enabled to tell me that his potman
frequently called at Mr. Smythe's house.

"Does he live in good style?" I asked.

"Oh yes, he is a good customer, and rather extravagant, but Nick Smythe has been known hereabouts for
years—a liberal-minded man, one of the best supporters of
local charities, and much respected."

I confess that I felt considerably damped by this description at the time—it pointed so conclusively, as I thought,
to Mr. Smythe's respectable position and to the danger of
injudicious interference with him. But after the affair of
the cheque, and when it was found that the handwriting
and signature corresponded with those of the documents
sent to Scotland Yard by complainants, we naturally asked
ourselves, "Who is Mr. Bruton? Is there a Bruton in the
firm?"

Our observation and persistent "shadowing" had made
us aware that the only persons to attend at the office in
Lincoln's Inn Fields regularly were Mr. Nicodemus Smythe
and his son, who acted as his clerk. In fact, we began to
share Mrs. Sairey Gamp's idea of Mrs. Harris, that "not
no such person" as Mr. Bruton existed.

In order to decide this matter conclusively, a colleague,
who was well versed in Italian and a knowledge of Italy,
and who had been during his career a civil engineer,
visited Mr. Smythe one morning and told the following
tale :—

"I have been travelling in Italy," he said, "and there
I became friendly with a civil engineer, to which profession
I belong This gentleman was known to me as Mr.

Bruton, but I have not seen him for some time. I never thought of seeing him again, for, unfortunately, I have lost his address.   On my return to London I looked up his name in the directory, and find that the only firm of Bruton and Co., civil engineers, is this one.   Can you tell me if I am not mistaken, for I should be glad to renew my old acquaintance with Mr. Bruton?"

My colleague thus addressed himself to Mr. Nicodemus Smythe, who replied, genially and courteously, that he was sorry to disappoint his visitor, but Mr Bruton was, well—ahem—in the country travelling for the sake of his health, and not expected back to business yet awhile, and so on.

This answer was sufficient for us, and as at that time we were working upon a very strong and specific complaint from Cork, we communicated with the Crown solicitor, strongly advising him to obtain a warrant.   He did so promptly, and we arrested Mr. Nicodemus Smythe at his elaborate offices in Lincoln's Inn Fields.

Upon a minute inspection of his books, which he had flaunted before me with so much effrontery, it was found that they were kept in such a manner as to deceive the outsider, but also to provide a record of swindling transactions by which not one farthing was advanced, and the income of Mr. Smythe had amounted to not less than six thousand pounds per annum.   I may say that the cheque which he had given the poor Irishwoman was very useful in showing that Smythe and Bruton and Co. were one and the same

Nicodemus was taken to Ireland, and the conviction was quashed, necessitating a new trial at enormous expense; but evidence accumulated, and the prisoner pleaded guilty.

His arrest opened up one of the largest inquiries I have ever had on hand, for it directed attention to other men who were carrying on loan-offices, and who also were advising their clients to patronize the Albion Assurance Company in Chancery Lane. The Treasury solicitor took the matter up, and it was my duty to investigate a great many complaints. It was almost an interminable task, and it was not easy to locate my men, for after the sentence passed upon Nicodemus, whom they knew very well, they were very cautious.

Three offices occupied my attention—one near to the British Museum, one off Holborn, and a third not far from Euston In the course of the inquiry it puzzled me very greatly to find that the handwriting on the documents proceeding from these three offices was apparently the same. Patient observation had shown that three brothers were engaged, one at each office, but they did not have any transactions with each other. The explanation of the similarity of handwriting, I afterwards found, was that the three brothers had been educated together at one school, and cultivated a resemblance of calligraphy.

Gradually, by dint of observation, coupled with "information received," we learned that a man known as "Timber Toes" was the principal, an extraordinary character, addicted to drinking champagne and to the wearing of lavender or rose-coloured kid gloves and big diamond studs.

He was a very difficult man to find, because he was so fond of society that he was accustomed to do the inquiry work himself, travelling up and down the country and ingratiating himself into the good books of his victims by inviting them to crack with him a small bottle of champagne. He had the air of a millionnaire, the heart of a philanthropist, and the open hand of a good fellow all round. After he had visited his clients there was seldom any difficulty raised by them about inquiry fees and so forth.

At the time "Timber Toes" was also a gambler, and associated with racing men, for he was the proprietor of a well-known gambling club at Brighton.

When "Timber Toes" was "wanted" he conveniently disappeared, and my attention was turned to the second man in the gang, and he being carefully "shadowed," led me in due time to No. 1.

That morning I was entirely alone, and when I had satisfied myself that "Timber Toes" and his assistant were comfortably located for some time at a gambling club, I gave a cabman an envelope to take to Scotland Yard asking for assistance, and waited until a colleague arrived, when we arrested the two men.

The connection between the "Timber Toes" set of loan offices with the Albion Assurance Office was as intimate as that which had existed between the latter and Nicodemus Smythe, *alias* Bruton and Co.

I found that the secretary of the Albion Assurance Office was apparently very respectable. I do not think he had at first realized that it was a bogus concern, but as none of the policies were renewed after the first year, the prosecution alleged that he must have had his eyes opened to the nature of the business. There was no board of directors, although there had been originally. The managing director, secretary, and clerks constituted the whole staff.

I

Warrants were out against all these men, and, having secured "Timber Toes ' and the second in command, I next proceeded to arrest the officials of the bogus assurance office, about which there was no difficulty.

Here I may state that the office had done an enormous business, and had regularly divided the premiums it received with the loan-office swindlers

Dowdell and Robson, two of my colleagues, then secured the others concerned in the three loan-offices, which was not an easy matter, as each capture which was effected made the rest of the gang more wary.

In one case the only clue to the whereabouts of a man called "The Captain" was obtained by "shadowing" a certain Government clerk of good position, but who was the associate of card-players, and was by them called "The Deaf Un." But "The Captain" was finally discovered and arrested.

At Bow Street Police Court an unfortunate thing occurred. It was the wretched old court which Dickens described in "Oliver Twist."

There were eight prisoners in the dock, and the court was crowded with their friends. The gaoler was very sleepy, and one of the prisoners was allowed out on bail, and speedily vacated the dock.

In order to make way for the prisoners to the cells it was necessary to force a road through the dense mass of humanity packed into the dingy court and completely surrounding the dock.

When the prisoners were counted in the cells, and allowing for the one let out on bail, the gaoler cried—

"There is one short!"

It was the man known as "The Captain," who had decamped, and he has never been seen from that day to this in London, for the warrant is still out against him

But how did he make good his escape? Very simply. In the press of the throng, as the prisoners were leaving the dock, "The Captain" ejaculated loud enough for the people to hear —

"Well, thank goodness my bail has been accepted."

And with these words he boldly mixed with his friends, and, without hindrance, speedily put as great a distance as possible between himself and the magistrate's court at Bow Street

CHAPTER XII.

MISTAKEN IDENTITY AND ITS DANGERS—HOW INNOCENT MEN HAVE BEEN ARRESTED.

PEOPLE often bear an astonishing resemblance to each other, and this similarity has sometimes been sorely perplexing and misleading to the detective. It is on record in the archives of Scotland Yard that a twin brother was once arrested, but he happened to be the wrong twin, and brought an action for false imprisonment.

There was, too, the case of the wooden-legged man who lived in a court—a *cul de sac*—and who was, one might think, easily to be identified; but when arrested he protested his innocence, saying—

"Yes, I know you want a wooden-legged man; but you see I've lost my *right* leg, and the man you want has lost his *left*. He lives next door to me up our court, and I saw him come home to-night. If you go to his house you will get him."

And sure enough the right—that is to say, the left—wooden-legged man was found.

The cases of mistaken identity which I shall now quote are from my own experience.

A very useful "auxiliary"—or, to give him the slang

title which is sometimes used, "a copper's nark"—brought me information about a noted burglar, "Little Jerry." I verily believe my auxiliary knew every burglar in London of any importance. The truth was that this man was concerned in racing, and associated with the lower class of betting men who congregate in public-houses, which are also used by the "crooks" or thieves.

I suppose a "nark" of this type has his own reasons for being on good terms with the police, at all events, we were often in the position to save him from trouble. I don't wish it to be understood that we connived at crime, but in every profession there is a certain amount of "give and take," and it was so in this instance.

Don't suppose, either, that an auxiliary gets highly paid by the detectives for his services. The fact is, the officer has to pay him out of his own pocket. Sometimes, but very rarely, official recognition may be obtained; but as a rule the "nark" is remunerated privately by the detective who engages him.

Now, as this has a bearing upon the question of rewards, let me here state that few officers in the service could maintain their position and keep in touch effectively with a necessarily large connection of acquaintances, any one of whom may suddenly become a most valuable ally, unless their pay was supplemented by "extras," in the shape of rewards or gratuities.

Although an auxiliary is content with little, in the course of the year the burden upon a detective's pocket is not small. It is fortunate that a "nark" finds his chief reward in the exercise of a native detective instinct which he cannot overcome.

Well, to my story. My auxiliary told me that "Little Jerry" was engaged in a series of burglaries, and was to be found in a certain locality.

A colleague joined me in a hunt for "Little Jerry," and without much difficulty we found out where he was living and watched him, with the object of "getting him out"— *i.e.* following him at night, whilst he should be engaged in one or other of his burglaries.

But it seemed to be out of the question to detect this man in the act of committing some crime.

He always succeeded in evading us. His house was so situated, in the midst of an East End rookery, that he could leave it without our knowledge. It was surrounded by a network of courts and alleys, which provided any number of outlets and inlets, and made the task of watching exceedingly difficult. There are many such intricate neighbourhoods still in East London, offering great facilities for criminals in hiding.

"Little Jerry," too, was a very artful man to follow. He would jump into railway trains on the move; get into a cab on one side and leave it on the other; slide into a public-house at one door and make his way out by the tap-room at the back; and, in fact, use all the tricks of the trade. In streets where men of his class dwell a stranger is quickly recognized, and should an unknown man enter a public-house the conversation is changed that instant.

It happened, however, that my auxiliary was able to supplement his information by the statement that "Little Jerry" was disposing of his "swag," or stolen property, to a certain receiver.

Now, a receiver is a very difficult bird to catch, and we

wished very much to capture both men—the receiver and the thief.

Not having succeeded in tracing "Little Jerry" at night, we altered our tactics and took to watching his lair by day, and, to our satisfaction, we were at last fortunate in "getting him out' one morning.

In order to do this we had recourse to an auxiliary This man called at "Little Jerry's" house, engaged him in conversation, and went out with him. The burglar never, of course, suspected the object of his friend's attentions.

The auxiliary did not long remain with "Little Jerry," who started off in a business-like way towards the City, and my colleague and I took up the trail. We were in the open street, but at some distance from each other, and were not discovered by our man.

His way led him to a City street of great respectability, to the address of the receiver—or "fence," as he would be called—whom we hoped to capture.

We allowed "Little Jerry" to remain in the house a few minutes, and then boldly walked up the staircase to the rooms of the "fence." This receiver had been suspected for years. However, the police possess no powers of search, and even if they have them, and the stolen property is found, the difficulty of getting it identified is so great that it is not often that a receiver is caught. He is usually "given away" by some man who "squeals" or incriminates his confederates out of revenge, or in the hope of lightening his own punishment.

We knocked, and the old man came to the door, and we then simply forced our way into his apartments, much to his surprise and terror.

There, at a table, on which was a great deal of jewellery, sat "Little Jerry" the burglar, with a pair of goldsmith's scales in front of him. In his hand he held a piece of Wedgwood (often used in assaying) upon which he had been rubbing some gold ornaments.

This Wedgwood is used instead of dropping the acid direct on the gold. The Wedgwood is so hard that a ⟨...⟩ of gold is soon rubbed off upon it, and the acid is then applied to this deposit. If it turns green it is a proof that the jewellery is "snide," in other words, not good

By this method the hacking about of the gold ornaments is saved Moreover, it happens that a gold-plating will resist acid, but cannot defy the rubbing.

The rooms were packed with the proceeds of burglaries. The receiver dwelt in the midst of these ill-gotten goods. He might have passed as an old curiosity dealer, which is a convenient "blind" for men of his class. Very often they combine a legitimate business with their nefarious trade, and are regular attendants at jewellery sales

We arrested both the receiver and the burglar, and I left my colleague in the room with the former while I conveyed "Little Jerry" into the street. I was anxious to return to my assistant as soon as possible, as he was alone with the receiver and so much stolen property.

Therefore I addressed myself to the first constable I met, and obtained his assistance. I handed him my prisoner.

"Hold him tight," I cautioned the policeman. "He is a very dangerous burglar. Take him to Bow Street police-station and ask the inspector to detain him until I bring the receiver we have also caught."

I then returned to the house, which we searched, and

calling a cab, we were about to take our prisoner to Bow Street with a quantity of stolen property.

But, as we were starting, my constable rushed back in breathless haste and panted—

"I beg your pardon, sir: I have lost the prisoner!"

"How did you do that?" we cried, whilst the old receiver audibly chuckled at our discomfiture.

"He begged me not to keep hold of him, sir," explained the chap-fallen constable. "He didn't want to be shown up, he said. He promised to walk quietly, and I thought he would. I let go my hold and directly afterwards he bolted. That's all, sir."

"Well, young man," said I, "I should not care to stand in your shoes."

The policeman, it afterwards appeared, had been in the force a few months only, but he did not look "green," or I should certainly not have trusted my prisoner to his charge. To lose a prisoner is considered a very serious matter in the service, and the constable was suspended from duty for a while, as a caution to be more careful in future.

Every effort was then made through our auxiliary to "pick up" our man—the escaped prisoner—again; but, although "Little Jerry" never suspected his betrayer, he did not fall into the trap a second time.

Finally, however, he was caught, his portrait in a police circular having attracted the attention of a divisional officer who knew "Little Jerry" the burglar well, and got information as to his whereabouts from another "nark."

A few weeks had elapsed after the escape of my prisoner, and the constable who had allowed him to regain his liberty

was restored to beat duty once more   He was patrol
ling the Thames Embankment, when suddenly he said to
a companion—

"Here is the man who got away from me !"

With that he seized a passer-by, crying—

"Halloa, I have found you at last !"

"What do you mean ?" demanded the person thus
accosted   "You might have found me when you liked."

"Oh ! that's all right. you will have to come along
with me."

"What for?" asked the individual, who seemed much
astonished

"You are the man who escaped from my custody a few
weeks ago,' said the constable, positively

"You have made a mistake," answered the stranger; "I
never was in your custody."

"Yes, you were.   Here, come along with me !" and he
seized his prisoner by the collar.

"Let me go !" begged the man, "and I'll walk quietly.
You need not show me up."

"Oh yes," retorted the policeman, with sarcasm, "that's
what you said before ; but I'm not going to be had
again."

So he marched him to Bow Street by the collar, and
reported to the inspector that he had captured "Little
Jerry," the escaped burglar.

Now, it happened that the divisional detective knew
"Little Jerry," and he came in at that moment to have a
look at the prisoner.

"Oh yes," said he . "that's 'Little Jerry,' right enough "

I chanced to call in at the police-station and saw the

man myself Certainly he was very like , but this man was not "Little Jerry."

"Oh yes; he's the man," said the inspector. "The divisional officer says so he has known 'Little Jerry' for years, and is perfectly satisfied that this man is he."

"Well," I answered, "I think I ought to know the man , but I may be mistaken as to the face There are, however, two tests which I should like to have applied. 'Little Jerry' may alter his appearance, but he cannot alter his walk and he can't change the tone of his voice "

The prisoner was asked some question, and I heard his answer, and was certain that the tone of his voice was not at all like that of "Little Jerry"

The man was then walked up and down, and I was further convinced that he could not be the burglar, as the gait differed.

Still they were not satisfied, for the opinions of the constable and of the local detective officer were against me. I suggested that my colleague should be asked to identify the prisoner, so a telegram was sent to the central office , and in the course of a little while he came to Bow Street

"No!" he exclaimed, having seen the prisoner , "he is not 'Little Jerry.'"

In the mean time I made some inquiry at the address which the man had given. It was a common lodging-house, and it was clearly established that he was not "Little Jerry," although, strange to say, he was an old thief. He certainly bore a very strong likeness to the burglar, and, in my opinion, the constable deserved great credit for bringing him in. He was, of course, released.

Now, in the second case which I shall mention, it may be thought incredible that a detective officer could make such a succession of mistakes; but, nevertheless, I admit that it was I who made them. It only proves how very careful a policeman should be in all matters of identification.

One day I was engaged in the neighbourhood of Islington, and jumped into a tram-car to return to the City, when I observed, as I supposed, seated on the top of an omnibus, journeying in the same direction, a man for whose arrest I held a warrant on a charge of fraud. I knew this man well, so I was careful to appear not to take the least notice of him, and as the omnibus and tram-car kept pretty close together I was able to follow him unobserved until we came to the end of the tram line.

I then took another omnibus and pursued my man, until he got off at the Bank.

I did not arrest him out of hand, because it was one of those cases in which it was necessary to find out where he lived, or where he would meet his confederates, for I believed he was working in partnership with another man.

Through the City, along Queen Victoria Street, as far as Blackfriars Bridge the man went, and I followed; but suddenly I lost him. He seemed to have dropped through the ground, and I could not account for his disappearance; and although I remained in the neighbourhood some time and searched a public-house close by, I could not find him.

Three weeks later I was walking along Queen Victoria Street, when in precisely the same spot where I had lost my man he reappeared.

A colleague was with me, and I said to him, "There is X., and I hold a warrant for his arrest."

I turned to the man and said, "Well, X., you know who I am. I am going to arrest you upon a warrant."

Frightfully scared, the man cried, "You know who I am? I don't know you!" and then began to run.

Immediately I seized him, and he cried out, "Police!" which I considered an extraordinary proceeding on his part.

The prisoner offered no explanation as to himself, but behaved as a guilty man. In fact, I believed that he was the man "wanted."

He was taken to the nearest City police-station, and there I ascertained in what way he had given me the slip three weeks before. The fact was, he had entered his father's place of business, and this gentleman came to the police-station and satisfactorily identified his son, who, I need hardly say, was not the man I wanted.

There could be no mistake—I had fallen into an error, and for that I was very much bullied, and my apologies were not regarded as sufficient. A voluminous official correspondence ensued, and although the man obtained no redress, as there was no malice on my part and the case was purely a question of mistaken identity, one would have thought that all the bother would have riveted the man's personal appearance upon my mind.

He did, indeed, haunt me as a nightmare.

Nevertheless, a little time afterwards I was again in Islington, looking for the man I wanted, when I saw him looking into a shop-window. I was sure that he was the very man for whose arrest I held a warrant. Yet before making him a prisoner, to be quite sure, I said to him, by way of precaution—

"How do you do?"

He turned, and replied curtly—

"I don't wish to have anything to say to you."

It was my friend the wrong man once more!

To complete this Experience I may state that eventually the right man was arrested, in consequence of his portrait having been inserted in the police "informations" which are circulated to all divisions of the Metropolitan Police District. This portrait was recognized by a detective, who was able to give me the clue to the man's whereabouts.

CHAPTER XIII.

COMPANIONS IN CRIME—A CRUSHED SIGNET RING GIVES
A CLUE.

IT is astonishing at times, in the investigation of robberies, how the one essential point which gives a clue
to the thief, or changes the venue of suspicion, is withheld
by those whose first duty it should be to give the information. This circumstance arises from many causes.

Sometimes it is due to sheer thoughtlessness or forgetful-
ness—synonymous terms in my opinion; sometimes to the
fear of its being thought suspicion is being cast in a wrong
quarter; and frequently the silence is kept with a view to
shielding the actual thief.

Of course these matters are very confusing to the officer,
often giving him endless trouble, always entailing waste of
time, and causing in many instances failure to elucidate
what, under the circumstances, remains a mystery but
might have been made quite clear.

Should the detective by any chance, in his questionings,
hit upon any piece of information he wants, and which has
not been forthcoming, "Oh!" says the witness, "I never
thought of it;" or, "I was afraid to mention it till you
asked me;" or, which more often happens, the individual

exclaims, "Oh! I did not think that was important." Certainly, it is quite true that what may become of much use to the officer often has no practical value to the minds of others.

Some of these difficulties presented themselves in a case which I was called upon to take up in the days before the Criminal Investigation Department was formed, and when it was customary in all heavy business for an officer to be sent from Scotland Yard to assist in such inquiries. This course was taken, not because the local officers were incapable of investigating crimes in their district, but because special matters frequently entailed much travelling, and it was not thought desirable to absent a local officer from the general and ordinary work of his division, always heavy enough, and demanding attention. His mind was, therefore, less free to undertake the working of a big case than if he had been unattached.

The number of the divisional detectives, as they were then called (for my part, I always liked the term "Detective Department" better than "Criminal Investigation Department"), was never too strong for the work of the division, so necessarily a local officer's actions were liable to be more fettered than those of his colleague from the central office.

A big burglary had been committed at a West End jeweller's shop and much property was missing. The discovery was made when the shutters were taken down in the morning.

From an inspection of the premises I satisfied myself that there was nothing to indicate that an entry had been effected by force, or that a "jemmy," or other tool used by thieves, had been employed.

The shop door was securely fastened, and no entrance could have been obtained in that way; but I realized that my difficulty rested in the door next to it, for it was a private one, opening into a passage leading to the living rooms, and there was also a door which shut off the shop

"Were these doors properly fastened?" I asked the assistant who was first to come downstairs on the morning of the discovery.

"I can't be certain. I didn't take particular notice," he replied, "but it's my impression they were not"

"Were the doors fastened last night?"

"I don't know,' the man replied

Although I could see no cause to cast suspicion upon any one, yet I felt convinced that some person then in the employ of the firm, or a discharged servant, must have had a hand in the robbery.

One day, having again taken stock of the premises, I suddenly noticed that the shutters were standing in the passage reached by the side door, and were not pushed up through the cellar grating, as is more frequently the case in old-fashioned shops.

This trifling detail suggested to me a possible clue. I waited until closing time at night. It was then very dark. I did not make known my presence, but as the shutters were being removed one by one from the passage by an assistant, I sidled up, and at last was successful in slipping into the passage without having been observed.

"Now," I argued, "if I can do this, the same plan of getting into the passage and thence into the shop may have been followed by the actual thief."

Still this difficulty remained: any ordinary thief might

K.

have done this, and, probably the jewellery having by this time gone into the receiver's melting-pot, what chance was there of bringing about a satisfactory identification?

"Where, too, is my evidence," I reflected, "even if some informant 'gives away' the thief, which is my only chance?"

But there was still the second solution: Was it possible that some discharged employé had stolen the jewellery, knowing how easy it would be for him to slip into the shop, as I had myself done?

I therefore pursued my inquiries in this direction, and on again questioning the jeweller, I learned from him facts which, up to that moment, he had not stated, perhaps because he did not think they had any bearing upon the case, or because he had forgotten them.

"Occasionally," said he, "an assistant employed in another branch of the business has in busy times helped in this shop."

"Where is he to be found?" I asked.

"He is not now in my employ," was the answer.

"What sort of character did you give him when he left your service?"

"I gave none at all. He was not well behaved."

Now, surely this matter was of the highest importance, and, having heard and taken note of this man's haunts and associates, I lost no time in hunting him up, and when found began to pay him some little attention.

Observation and information are the detective's two best weapons. In this case I resolved to watch the discharged assistant quietly. It is certainly true that a man is known by the company that he keeps.

On one occasion I found my man in the company of another, whose looks, and more particularly his manner, aroused all my detective instinct.

I resolved to leave the assistant for the time to amuse himself in a low place of entertainment to which he was accustomed to resort, and to "shadow" instead his friend.

It was not long before I saw him in a quarter of the town which went far to warrant my suspicions that he was "a bad lot"

Further inquiry concerning this man strengthened my ideas of him and his vocation, and at the same time I opened up an inquiry into the antecedents of the ex-assistant, who was, at this time, out of employ.

In the course of this investigation I gathered much useful information, and fell into the path of a young fellow who had worked with the jeweller's assistant.

"He seemed to have a good crib," said the man, "and one day he showed me a gold watch—a stunner. His employers gave it to him as a testimonial, and his old pals gave him some gold links and things."

It appeared that the display of these articles had been made a few days after the robbery. Of course, the jewellery might have been honestly acquired; and as the former employers of the shop-assistant gave him a "fair" character, I had to exercise considerable caution in proceeding.

"Shall I arrest him on the off-chance of finding some of the stolen property in his possession?" I asked myself.

No, this would be too risky; for should none of the jewellery be found there would be no evidence against him, as the allegation that he had shown a watch to a friend provided, after all, merely a suspicion that he was concerned in the larceny, and certainly was not sufficient to deprive a British subject of his liberty.

To arrest a man whose character is indifferent without a case against him is bad, but to arrest a man of "fair" character is worse, and actions for wrongful imprisonment are not unknown.

I set down these reflections as they occurred to me at the time, for they will, perhaps, open up to the minds of many people the nature of the difficulties with which an officer of justice has to contend in working his cases to a successful issue

Now, the plan which I decided to adopt was to place this discharged shop-assistant under unmistakable observation, to make no secret that he was watched by the police I wanted to see what effect this "shadowing" would have upon him, for I have never known a guilty person who could submit to this espionage, as you may call it, with equanimity, and, moreover, it affects the innocent, too, sometimes very curiously. The effect in either case is marked, and it either tends to strengthen suspicion by producing positive proofs, or relieves the innocent of an impending charge

In this case the end speedily justified the means, for immediately the man discovered that detectives were manifesting curiosity as to his movements he was in a terrible fright. He appeared to lose all control of himself, and fell into such vacillation whilst walking about that he evidently forget his destination—everything pointing to the workings of a guilty conscience.

The poor fellow would twist and turn about a few times in a vague attempt to remove the "shadow," but then would resign himself to a rash flight; for he could stand the spying no longer.

Now, this condition of mind was exactly what I desired and expected.

I gave chase, but the run was not a long one, as the "race was to the swift," and in those days I could cover the ground well.

As the man started I had observed him put his hand to his mouth, as though he proposed taking something from it, and the next action suggested that he had thrown something into a garden in front of a house in which there was a grass plot On overtaking him I determined to arrest him on suspicion, in the belief that he had been concerned in the jewel robbery.

But when at the nearest police-station I proceeded to search my prisoner I found upon him not a vestige of evidence—no jewellery, and very little money; the latter fact, to my mind, giving ground for hope that the proceeds of the robbery had not been realized

Leaving my prisoner at the station, I returned to the house which we had passed, and began a search of the grass plot I have mentioned, having first gained the necessary permission from the occupiers, without, however, disclosing my object.

"Hello, wot's up?" cried one passer-by, keenly interested in our movements. "Wot d'ye expect to find—mother-in-law's money?"

The hunt, fortunately, was not a protracted business; for in a little while I raked out of the grass a signet ring.

It was crushed out of shape, and bore the marks of powerful jaws and teeth.

This ring, naturally, I considered to be a valuable piece of testimony, and when I submitted it to the prosecutor he at once identified it as a portion of the stolen jewellery.

But we were still at a loss to discover the hiding-place of the "swag;" and a search of the prisoner's lodgings disclosed no clue. Evidently the man had an accomplice. Who was it?

My thoughts and suspicions reverted to the fellow I had seen in the assistant's company; and, as far as my powers with regard to the questioning of prisoners would allow me, I endeavoured to draw my man out upon the subject; but his replies to hints, insinuations, and direct interrogation, when that was possible, were so shifty and hesitating, that I determined to take the bull by the horns and "go for" the other man.

By this time it was growing very late, and at that time of night much caution was necessary, owing to the class of people who lived in the street in which this individual resided. Luckily there were excellent facilities to enable me to keep near to his house almost unseen.

I sent a small boy to this house with a message to the man, saying that "a friend" was waiting for him at a neighbouring public-house, knowing that he would suppose this friend to be the assistant who was in custody at the police-station.

"He is out," said the lad, as he came back with the reply, "and he mayn't be 'ome afore midnight;" and this intelligence was what I wanted.

There was one thing to be feared. It was possible that the man, returning home, might secure the door in such a way as to make an entrance difficult; for, although I noticed that none of the lodgers were at all particular about shutting the front door, it was probable that the last man to come home would fasten it.

To get over that difficulty I plugged a piece of wood on the threshold so that the door would not properly close.

Then, with my assistant, I waited in the shadow for the home-coming of our man.

At last the rays of the street lamp fell upon him, accompanied by a woman. They entered the house, and we allowed them sufficient time to settle down, to make sure of the stolen property being in their possession.

The front door was not quite shut, and we opened it easily and ascended the stairs with as little noise as possible.

The door of the room occupied by the man was unfastened, and we simply walked in, a bull's-eye borrowed from a constable who was on the scene enabling us to take a survey of the apartment.

Our intrusion was so sudden and unexpected, and our man jumped up with such energy and astonishment, that I thought he meant to fight, and I threw myself into a pugilistic attitude of defence; but he saw that I was not alone, and gave in

The light of the bull's-eye shone upon rings, brooches, and ear rings heaped on the mantelpiece, and a new watch ticked on the table. I seized these, and afterwards found that they were some of the stolen jewellery.

More articles of the same kind were found in the room, and although this recovery was satisfactory as far as it went, the bulk of the property was still missing, a few pawn tickets, however, explaining the absence of some of it.

Acting upon my experience that a thief never gives a detective credit for the making of an arrest upon detective principles alone, but always imagines that it is "from information received" from some "pal" who has "rounded" on him, I set about to extract "a squeal" (confession implicating other men) from one of the prisoners, this man believing that a confederate had betrayed him.

In this way I obtained the name and address of another accomplice, and started off afresh

My colleague and I betook ourselves to the address given, and frightened the landlady of the house by our late call, but she told us in which room the man we wanted was sleeping. The door, however, was fast, and evidently the man had been disturbed, for I heard sounds within the room.

There was a certain scraping, scratching noise, as though a body was being dragged across the floor. Then the window was cautiously lifted.

At once I hurried to the back door, although we had put a man on guard in that direction, to provide for any attempted escape at the rear. Reaching the yard, I heard the window above me closed, and then came a shout from my colleague.

Hastening to the room again, I found that he had gained access to the room and secured the prisoner.

We searched the place well, but no jewellery was found.

"Never had none!" declared the man persistently, protesting his innocence.

"But why," I thought, "should this man want to go to the window?"

Taking a bull's-eye, I renewed the hunt and raised the sash.

Just outside the window was the coping of a flat-roofed outhouse, and on the stonework was a box. It was this box, no doubt, which I had heard dragged from its place of concealment beneath the bed and pushed out of the window.

We opened the box, and in it were gold and silver watches, rings, pins, brooches, ear-rings, chains, and, in fact, all of the property, with the exception of about £40 worth, represented by the pawn tickets, and, curiously enough, these articles had been pledged at a branch establishment of their lawful owner, notwithstanding that the particulars of the stolen goods had been carefully circulated to him in the usual manner.

It was a pleasant sight, not only to me, but afterwards to the man who had been robbed of them, to gaze upon these valuable goods.

All that remained to be done was to search the thief. He was the man who had been secreted in the jeweller's shop by the dishonest assistant. Upon him I discovered a singular document. It was a carefully drawn inventory of the stolen goods, prepared so that it was not possible for the thieves to defraud each other of their unlawful gains

In this inventory, gold watches were described as "red herrings," silver ditto as "fresh herrings," chains as "sprats," rings as "whelks," ear-rings as "winkles," brooches as " haddocks," and so on—to the end

.

CHAPTER XIV

HOW FORGERS BAFFLE DETECTIVES—THE FORGER KING
MAKES STARTLING DISCLOSURES.

PROBABLY there has been no criminal during the last quarter of a century who has given the detective police—not only those of the metropolitan force and of the City of London, but those also of the provinces and of Ireland—so much work to do as the notorious forger, William Walters, the king of a very dangerous gang of "cheque-raisers."

This man surrounded himself with a "school" of willing and able assistants, but it was his fertile brain that concocted schemes and directed the operations in carrying them out. The members of the "mob" regarded him as a genius and looked up to him as their leader.

Walters was not an hereditary criminal. He was the son of a hotel proprietor in a racing county, and the house kept by his father was largely patronized by racing and stable men. When Walters senior died, and the widow continued the business, her only boy naturally drifted into the company of the men who frequented the hotel, and gradually he fell into association with sharpers

The mother gave up the hotel to share the fortunes of her son, came to London with him, and followed him to America. He had been concerned in the earlier Turf Frauds, for which he was prosecuted, but when released on bail he absconded to the States. But he did not remain there.

In common, as I have hinted, with most detective officers in the United Kingdom, Walters kept me pretty busy, although at the time I did not know that it was his hand which was finding me work to do.

At the time of which I speak startling forgeries in quick succession were alarming the whole country. The mode of operation was briefly this. A cheque would be obtained for a small amount from a legitimate dealer or tradesman, the figures would then be altered to represent a large sum, and the draft would be taken to the bank by a dupe, or messenger, and cashed.

Of course, after each repetition of this manœuvre bankers became very much on their guard, and the police were on the alert to catch the forger.

I had, myself, a case in which it was early suspected that expert hands were at work. My plans to capture them were very elaborate. I was secreted in the bank, and I thought I was fairly safe, as I had made arrangements for quitting it by a side entrance, which would lead me into another street, directly the forged cheque was presented for payment, by which ruse I hoped to be able to follow the messenger, unperceived by him or his associates.

Thus concealed in a private part of the bank premises I awaited developments.

A bogus cheque was one day handed to the teller, the

forgery was detected, but nothing was said, and the money was duly paid by the cashier.

I received a signal to notify me such had been the case, and leaving the bank by the side door started in pursuit, but when I emerged into the open street I found that none of the gang were anywhere to be seen, and it was then clearly evident to me that the "shadower" had himself been shadowed. That is to say, I had myself been under observation on the part of the spies of the gang, and the side street had been "blocked" by them. They must have seen me come out of the bank.

On another occasion a dummy parcel of cash was made up in readiness to give to the person who presented the forged cheque, but the dodge seemed to have been immediately detected, and when I came upon the scene no traces of the forgers could be found, although I was successful in following the messenger who carried the bogus money to the rendezvous, but he was greatly confused when no one came to meet him as arranged; for at the first alarm the gang had dispersed.

In a third case, in order to avoid arousing suspicion, I planned never to go near the bank at all, but received the signal that a forged cheque had been presented by noting that a piece of paper had been pasted on the window of the bank by the manager within. Even then I failed to arrest any member of the gang

Some time later than the incidents to which I have referred, the whole of the plans of Walters (who had been betrayed to the police by a companion in crime) came to my knowledge almost at first hand, for Walters had divulged them to a confederate.

As I venture to think they will be of great interest, not only to bankers and to the public generally, but also to the police of England and America, I will here set down in some detail the revelations which up to this moment have never been made public.

In carrying out a forgery, the first step of the gang was to obtain a cheque which might be "raised" to a greater value

Now, this was done in different ways. In one case, an auctioneer at York held a large sale of horses, and a member of the Walters gang having taken lodgings in the city, bought a horse, and afterwards explained that the friend for whom he had purchased it did not approve of the animal, and therefore requested the auctioneer to sell it again. This the latter did, and duly gave his cheque for the horse, but as this cheque was printed in fugitive colours it could not be altered.

A few weeks later one of Walters's "pals," L——, suggested that a customer should be followed from a certain bank—the same at which the auctioneer had an account—and if he turned out to be a tradesman his signature should be obtained by making a purchase of him and getting his receipt. Accordingly L——, having watched a milliner's boy to and from this bank in York—the boy was carrying a pass-book, a bad tell-tale—another of the gang forged the milliner's name to an order for a cheque-book, and duly received it

This man, B——, then took apartments, engaged a clerk, and sent him to the bank with a forged cheque.

It was Walters himself who forged this cheque, and he imitated the signature of the auctioneer badly, for the bank

authorities discovered that it was a fraud, and sent round
to the customer, saying that the signature differed.

On that occasion B—— was very nearly arrested, and
he left his umbrella behind him at his apartments in the
hurry of his flight.

As I have not the space here to enter into other cases,
I may say that the work of the gang appeared to have been
thus divided. B——, or else R——, obtained the cheques,
Walters altered them, and L—— did the watching, whilst
some poor dupe—a clerk, a boy, or casual messenger—
once it was the driver of a brougham—was selected to cash
the cheque, meanwhile being kept under close observation
by members of the gang.

Before narrating incidents which will further elucidate
the business I will now let Walters himself explain, in his
own language, how a cheque is "raised." His first forgery
was committed at Montreal, and L—— was then with him
They met there by appointment an old hand—I. M.——,
and the proceeds of the forgery carried out by them
amounted to 500 dollars (£100)

"I gave M——," said Walters to his friend, "twenty-five
dollars to show me how to raise or alter a cheque, which
he did.

"Perhaps it may be interesting to you to know how the
chemicals are mixed. Put into a pint and a half bottle
about five and a half ounces of bicarbonate of soda and
fill it up with water, leaving room to shake it well up for
five minutes. Then let it stand for an hour. Get a two-
ounce bottle and put in it not quite a small teaspoonful of
chloride of lime, and fill it up from the bottle containing
the bicarbonate of soda water. Shake it well for five

minutes and then let it stand until the chloride of lime has sunk to the bottom.

" If the liquid turns a pale pink it is of the right strength ; if to a dark pink, then the soda is too strong (but that is not very material) ; if the liquid turns yellow the lime is too strong, and would discolour the paper."

" How long does it take to alter a cheque?" asked the confederate.

" Two hours," answered Walters " The lime-and-soda mixture is applied with a camel's-hair brush, and after it has eaten up or destroyed the ink it has to be well washed off with water, otherwise the mixture would destroy the paper Then the cheque has to be left to dry naturally, not by any artificial heat, or the paper will curl, and after it is thoroughly dry it has to be painted over with a solution of isinglass and water, so as to prevent the ink from running when the cheque is rewritten."

" What is the way to make the solution of isinglass ? "

" You put about the sixth part of an ounce into a small teacup and pour on it boiling water," replied the Forger King. " It should be used when it is nearly cold, and when quite cold, if of the proper strength, it should form a jelly. The cheque should be rubbed flat between two sheets of paper before it is refilled in.

" Do you want to hear how I learned to forge a name?" continued Walters in his communicative mood. " Henry H—— told me, and he was taught by a man named R——. The method is as follows:—Trace over the signature with a pen and ink or pencil on a piece of tracing-cloth or tracing-paper. Then by applying the tracing to a window and putting a cheque or piece of writing-paper over it you can with a fine lead pencil obtain the exact facsimile of the signature or handwriting required, which you afterwards must ink over with a fine pen "

Now, I have chosen to quote Walters as an exact authority upon these methods, but it is only fair to allow him to continue, and warn the public how they are to tell a signature that has been forged.

"The pencil-marks under the ink," declared Walters to his companion, "give a much duller appearance than the other part of the cheque, and through the magnifying glass the strokes and writing are seen to have a jagged, shaky-looking appearance. And if a forgery has been committed on a blank sheet of paper it will be found that the est of the handwriting is quite different from that of the signature, and unless carefully rubbed out, the pencil-marks can be seen with the aid of a glass, or the surface of the paper will have been injured by the use of indiarubber.

"Then how are you to tell an altered cheque? In this way: When chemicals have been applied the ink will have a very peculiar black appearance, and in all cases, by holding the cheque in a certain position, one can easily perceive where the solution of isinglass has been applied. This solution will also have a lot of bright unnatural sparkles, and through a magnifying glass the surface of the paper will be seen to have been disturbed and injured."

I do not think that this system of "raising" cheques is now practised, and bankers must be thankful that Walters is in penal servitude for life. The forgers were at the pains sometimes to procure ink of the same kind as that used by the firm whose cheque they intend to raise. In one case, so my informant was told, F—— altered a cheque, Walters pencilled in the words "hundred and five pounds" and the figures £905. F—— filled in the signature and B——, having a steadier hand than Walters, went over his pencilling.

"If the banks used only fugitive c.   o ordinary forger could alter them," Walters once .   , and it is clear that the gang were often put to a great c d of trouble in procuring cheques to raise, only to discover that, because they were printed in colours which disappeared when the acid was applied, they could not be safely tampered with, and therefore the cheques were cashed in the ordinary course

"In the United States," Walters stated one day, "most banks use patent paper. If this were made pink no forgery or altering a cheque could occur, except by some very skilled hand This pink paper turns white directly any chemical touches it. As a rule chemicals will not take out blue ink."

To these disclosures it may be interesting to add that amongst the tools employed by Walters and his confederates were fine pens to ink over the pencilled forged signatures; camel's-hair brushes—four or five, and perhaps more, were required to alter a cheque, for the chloride of lime quickly spoilt the brush, a boy's trumpet, used as a funnel, some patent sizing, to take the place of isinglass, only it was found that it left a brown stain, a magnifying glass with which to examine the erasures; and coloured crayons and paints, to restore the colour of a cheque, if destroyed, but it was discovered that they were not successful, bogus bill-heads and address cards.

Blank cheques, it appeared from further admissions made

by the Forger King, were sometimes stolen, once from the pocket of a cattle-dealer, and on another occasion by some "hooks" or pickpockets, who stipulated for a share of the proceeds of the robbery.

A cheque obtained in the course of business would frequently, at request, be made payable to an "Alfred Hunderwood," because the first four letters of the surname and the last three of the Christian name supplied the complete word "hundred," which was so convenient to copy in the "raising" of the value of the cheque. Similar names were occasionally adopted.

In these preliminary transactions capitalists were needed, and the persons who found the money for a notorious Birmingham affair were D. N——, an American, and a man known to the police as "Jimmy."

I have quoted my own experiences to show how successful the forgers usually were in making good their escape from the banks after the perpetration of one of their *coups*, although the forgery might be discovered at once. They ran some narrow risks, and it may not be out of place now to mention one or two of Walters's failures.

A publican, having an account at a London branch bank, at King's Cross, was marked down, and B—— obtained his cheque for £2 5s., payable to Alfred Hunt, this name having been selected for the reason I have already enlarged upon. The cheque, however, was printed in fugitive colours, and as it could not be altered, it was cashed at the bank by L——. B—— then procured from another licensed victualler a blank cheque on the same bank, and Walters forged the signature of the first publican.

The next move was for B—— to take apartments in

Gower Street under the name of Hunt, and to advertise for a clerk. A bogus cheque was intentionally left upon a table when a likely applicant answered the advertisement in person. It was drawn for a decent sum. to impose upon the young man and give him an idea of the financial standing of his new employer, for the clerk was duly engaged.

Amongst his very first duties was an errand to the bank, in order that he might cash the forged cheque, and meanwhile L——, "made up" as a respectable old gentleman, with gold-rimmed specs, kept watch upon the clerk's movements from a convenient spot inside the bank, pretending to have business there at a counter.

When the cheque was presented L—— observed that something was amiss No money was given by the cashier to the clerk, and the manager, having been consulted, said to the messenger—

"We shall have to see Mr. Hunt about this cheque. Where does he live?"

"In Gower Street," answered the clerk, and gave the number.

"Very well; I shall send some one to see him," said the manager

Of course this was enough for L——, the watcher; and the bank porter was a little at a loss to know why the respectable old gentleman in gold glasses should be in such a hurry to leave the premises; but no one else took any notice of the incident.

L—— lost no time in communicating with B—— at Gower Street, and the latter was in such haste to escape that this time he left his gold watch behind him on the table, to share the fate of his lost umbrella.

Just about the same time B—— obtained another cheque —also a publican's—and he altered it, endorsed it, and handed it to a West End money-changer to pass through his account. In this case the cheque was payable to "S H Hunter," which name gave the combination of letters for the first part of the word "hundred," the draft being altered to the amount of £200 10s.

B—— represented to the money-changer that he was S. H. Hunter, of Fitzroy Square, and presented an engraved card (bogus, of course) bearing this name and address.

Now, the point which the rogues desired to learn was whether it was safe for B—— to call upon the money-changer for the cash, and L—— suggested that some money should be sent to the publican, asking him to oblige with another cheque.

If the cheque should be given the forgers would then conclude that everything was right; so B—— sent a lad with money to the publican, and L—— went into the public-house and watched the boy.

L—— then observed a man, whom he imagined to be a detective, and he saw the landlord and this officer go to the bank, but not to the public entrance.

They rang the side-door bell, and then L—— decided that the forgery must have been discovered, and went at once to warn his confederate, B——, of the fact, and both men made good their escape.

I could multiply such instances, on the strength of "information received," of the manner in which forgers have succeeded in baffling detectives—myself among the rest.

CHAPTER XV.

A "PLANT" UPON PAWNBROKERS—HOW THE SWINDLERS
PUZZLED THE POLICE.

IN the last chapter I have referred to the extremely cunning manner in which Walters, the Forger King, and his associates, carried out a succession of forgeries upon London and other banks, baffling detectives in the most tantalizing manner.

Before proceeding to relate another case—unfortunate, in the sense that I was completely nonplussed by the same gang, then working in another department of crime—I wish to place on record, from the notes supplied to me by a useful "auxiliary," the methods by which Walters was enabled, in one particular instance, to circumvent us all in his favourite line of forgery.

Although the information which I now give was of that nature known as "received," in contradistinction to that which is "obtained" by actual detective work, it should be none the less enlightening, as it gives some idea of the advantage which Scotland Yard derives from outside informants, apart from the diligence of its own officers.

A very clever swindler—it would be hard to find his

equal—a man I shall call L——, by careful inquiry ascertained that Y. Z. and Co., a certain firm of meat salesmen in Smithfield Market, had an account at a well-known bank in the immediate neighbourhood. By means of a sale of some harness to this firm, he obtained their cheque for £2 5s., payable to a Mr. Huntley, of Portland Road, W.

At Portland Road another member of the gang then took apartments, passing under the name of Alfred Huntley.

A variation in the usual procedure was at this point introduced into the plot. Huntley went down to Richmond, and there, calling himself by the name of Mr. Y. Z , and pretending to be a member of the meat salesmen's firm at Smithfield, took rooms. He had now two addresses and two *aliases*. In London he was Mr. Huntley, of Portland Road, and in Richmond, Mr. Y. Z., of the Meat Market.

One day a solicitor of Lincoln's Inn Fields was visited by a gentleman, who requested him to sue a Mr. Y. Z , of Richmond, for a debt due to Mr. Huntley, of Portland Road. The new client, who was none other than the forger, S——, then passing as Huntley, produced letters—all of them fabricated—purporting to have been sent by Mr. Y. Z. to him with reference to the sum that was owing.

The solicitor thereupon wrote "a lawyer's letter" to the man who would not pay up—Mr. Y. Z., of Richmond—and S——, the forger, coolly proceeded to Richmond and received the letter himself.

This letter S—— handed to Walters and his confederate, the smart L——, and at the latter's suggestion the Forger King wrote a reply to it, to which the forged signature of Mr. Y. Z., the meat salesman, was appended.

Other correspondence ensued, and the signature of the

unwitting meat salesman was continually used, so that it must have become pretty familiar to the Lincoln's Inn solicitor.

It was in this way that the ground was carefully prepared, and at last came the *coup*.

It was pretended by the gang that Mr. Y Z., of Richmond, in fear of legal proceedings in the courts, suddenly resolved to pay his pressing creditor, Mr Huntley, of Portland Road. Accordingly, one day a letter was posted at Richmond, containing a cheque for the amount of the fictitious debt— £600.

That cheque was forged, the original cheque, obtained from Messrs. Y. Z. and Co., of Smithfield, having been skilfully altered or "raised," the figures and writing having been obliterated by the use of chemicals, and new words and figures filled in.

It was arranged that S——, posing in his character of the creditor Huntley, should call upon his solicitor at a time when the Richmond letter would have been received. He did so, and asked of the lawyer—

"Well, sir, how is my little affair progressing? Has the man Y. Z. come to his senses yet, or have I still to wait for my money?"

"No, Mr. Huntley," replied the solicitor, rubbing his hands gleefully, "a little gentle pressure has succeeded People say we lawyers only have an eye to costs, and so on, but it isn't true. Our clients' interests are our own interests."

"Do you mean to say," cried the scamp, with marvellous self-possession—"do you mean to tell me that you have got the money?"

"Yes, sir, I do, and here it is"

And with that he produced the forged cheque sent from Richmond, signed by Y Z. and Co, and drawn in favour of Mr. Alfred Huntley.

Huntley took the cheque, and then said, "You're a reliable man, sir, I shall certainly recommend you to my friends. But there is one other favour——"

"What can I do for you?" said the lawyer, intensely gratified

"Well, I'm just off to the Isle of Wight, to my country place, by the two train, my cab is waiting at the door. I don't think we ought to lose time in clearing this cheque. You see it's crossed. If I pay it in to my Ryde account, we shall lose a day or so in the post. Would you oblige me by paying the cheque to the credit of your own account, and then you can remit me the amount, deducting your costs, at your convenience?'

"Oh, certainly," said the solicitor

"And, by-the-by," said Mr. Huntley, as he bustled to the door to his cab, "you can address me to Portland Road, for I shall be back in town to-morrow. Let me know when the cheque is cleared, will you?"

"Quite so," said the solicitor

Huntley did not go to the Isle of Wight, but to Richmond, to await the clearing of the crossed cheque, to which end all this scheming had tended

In due course the solicitor wrote to Portland Road, but he did not send the money. He asked that Huntley would send or call for it, as a question had arisen about the receipt which was to be given to Mr. Y. Z. for the payment of the debt.

Huntley chanced to come across a man that morning who hailed from Chatham, and he employed this fellow as his messenger. He sent him to Lincoln's Inn Fields, and the lawyer wrote in reply, requesting Huntley to send again later in the day.

L——, the member of the gang upon whom devolved most of the watching, was meanwhile keeping the lawyer's office under observation, and he noticed that the messenger returning with the lawyer's letter to Huntley was being followed by detectives

Huntley was waiting in a public-house in Chancery Lane, and L—— immediately went to him and gave him the alarm. The pair had soon left the neighbourhood of London, and neither Huntley at Portland Road nor Mr Y. Z. at Richmond was ever seen again

The police will probably remember that in this case the unsuspecting messenger was arrested, charged at Bow Street Police Court, remanded for a week, and then discharged by Mr. Flowers, the magistrate, as having played a perfectly innocent share in the transaction.

It must be obvious that a scheme of this kind, involving much time and expense in carrying it out, could never have been attempted without there had been a capitalist behind it. Hurry in the development of such a plan of fraud spells failure, and time costs money. But capital is never wanting.

There are numbers of men of means who are prepared to invest or speculate in the working out of some good idea, propounded by rogues of the Walters type.

These financiers may stand to lose as much as £1000 before any profit is divisible

The capitalists do not themselves thieve, or forge, or plan crimes, and, at the most, their connection with crime, beyond finding the sinews of war at the onset, is limited to the purchase or negotiation of stolen bonds or other property; but these are the men who make riches out of the business, and who, as a rule, escape the penalties of their misdeeds.

A capitalist must have been at the back of a very ingenious fraud which Walters and his friends successfully practised upon London pawnbrokers. This case concerned me closely, as I have to reckon it amongst my failures.

Walters was the headpiece of the swindlers, and his satellites simply pulled the chestnuts out of the fire. Walters himself ran very little risk.

Capital was required in this instance for the purchase of some very handsome and valuable articles of jewellery. Having obtained these, Walters next made a selection of the very best pawnbrokers in the metropolis, firms which are accustomed to advance considerable sums upon plate, etc., at special rates.

One of the swindlers would then take a piece of jewellery, valued at perhaps £50 or £60—or a gold watch and chain—or diamond ring, and pledge it with one of the selected pawnbrokers.

A fortnight or three weeks later, this same member of the gang would redeem the article, and immediately take it to another pawnbroker and there pledge it afresh. Perhaps with this man he had pawned a brooch, and he would take the brooch out, saying he wanted it for a present, and then immediately go to the first pawnbroker and ask for an advance upon it.

There was no fraud in this part of the game; it was simply ground-baiting; and all the time the capitalist was discharging the expenses of the gang, paying the interest on the pawn-tickets, etc.

Meanwhile the men— for there were several—who were thus engaged in pawning and repawning the jewellery, were gradually ingratiating themselves into the good opinions of the firms whom they patronized, and finally, when the time had arrived, they would tell a story more or less of this character .—

"Those infernal lawyers," one man would say, "take an awful long time in settling up affairs. Here am I, with plenty of money locked up in an estate I can't handle until they've settled succession duty and probate, and all that kind of thing I am awfully short of cash, as you can see; and it's lucky I have got this jewellery to raise a little money upon. I have had to pawn the family plate, too; that was made over to me as a gift, so I had that without trouble when my uncle died. Good old chap. Not much plate, though."

"We haven't any of it, have we, sir, in charge for you?"

"No, that's up in Scotland. Awfully high interest those Scotchmen want. By the way, what do you charge on plate?"

The pawnbroker named a special rate.

"That's very much lower than they want in Edinburgh," commented his client; "what a pity it was I did not let you have it !"

"How much is there of it?" asked the pawnbroker.

"Oh, about £200 worth. I mean, that is the amount of the loan."

"Why don't you get it transferred to London?"

"Can I do that?" eagerly asked the customer

"Certainly you can All you have to do is to bring us the deposit notes, and we will communicate with the pawnbrokers in Edinburgh, ascertain what interest is due, and arrange to have it transferred here"

"Thanks. I shall be awfully glad if you will."

The swindler then hurried to his colleagues. A man was despatched post haste to Edinburgh, with instructions to pass as Mr. McCall. Deposit notes which had been printed in readiness were filled in and forged.

Exactly the same procedure was followed in other cases, for the scheme was to victimize not one pawnbroker, but several at one *coup*, as it would never have done to allow any one failure to prejudice the chances of success in other directions.

In a day or two, all arrangements having been carefully made, the swindlers who had been delegated to perform this part of the work took to the respective pawnbrokers the bogus deposit notes, which were all properly prepared in due form, and they were told that the necessary communications would be made with Edinburgh.

"Much obliged for your promptitude," the swindler would say; "when do you expect to hear from the Scotchman, McCall?"

"Say the day after to-morrow."

"That will do nicely."

By the return post from Edinburgh came in due course a properly printed form, stating that such and such plate had been pledged, according to the terms of the advice, and that the interest amounted to so much.

"Upon receipt of your cheque," McCall wrote, "I shall be happ to meet your views and transfer the property to London."

It may seem incredible, but upon the faith of such documents several pawnbrokers put down at once bank-notes; and although some gave cheques, and one or two took the precaution to post-date them, and thereby saved a loss, it remains a fact that the rogues secured £1200 by their clever trick, and were not arrested.

I myself had the investigation of the whole affair. All that I had to work upon was the description of men who had pawned the jewellery, and of a man who had been seen in Scotland, but the details were very ordinary. All my usual sources of information failed me; and, I confess, it was not until Walters was in custody for his forgeries that I knew that he had been the prime mover in this "plant" upon pawnbrokers.

Before I conclude this experience, having specially referred to the kind of man who conceives and directs crime, I am reminded of another very notorious criminal, now languishing in a Continental prison, who put up many "jobs." I shall have occasion to refer a little later to some of his most sensational achievements, but for the present I quote his case in proof of the falsity of the adage that there is "honour among thieves."

The man of whom I speak, whose criminal capacities and inventive genius were certainly not inferior to those of Walters, acquired the reputation of having got the best of everybody in his line with whom he ever had transactions.

It was his policy to deal with weak men, whereas one of

Walters's colleagues (L——) was almost the equal of his chief in cunning.

Harry X——, as I shall call this other rogue of the first water, never recognized the principle of fair dealing, and he invariably took advantage of his "pals," as perhaps he felt entitled to do, as the head and soul of every job.

Thus, in the case of a famous American bank robbery, he is suspected of having "weeded the swag" to the amount of nearly £10,000. In a diamond robbery, effected in Paris, he defrauded his confederate by purchasing "off-colour" diamonds, substituting them for others of the first quality which were amongst the spoil, thereby reducing the value of his colleague's share by one-half—another instance of "weeding the swag."

CHAPTER XVI.

CAPITAL : TEN SHILLINGS—THE MANOR HOUSE AND OTHER FRAUDS.

MR. SMEE SKEFFINGTON SMEE was one of the most ingenious swindlers I have ever met. I made his acquaintance in this way. Numerous complaints were sent to Scotland Yard of an individual who had obtained goods from various tradesmen, and had decamped without paying their bills. He had addressed his orders from "The Manor House," at W——.

I went down to W——. The Manor House was a fine, old-fashioned place, a beautiful retreat, and as it adjoined the churchyard, I imagined that at one time it had been the vicarage. It was quite deserted when I arrived there, and in its rooms, which had, however, been recently occupied, there was no furniture, except that which belonged to the owner.

I made inquiries in the neighbourhood, and learned that the late tenant, Mr Smee Skeffington Smee, had occupied the place for a few months, but he had left as he had come, with his wife, two children, and a few bandboxes. He was in debt to several of the tradespeople, but they had not refused him credit, for he lived on the system of what is called partly paying your debts. He would run up an account for £10, pay the tradesman £5, and the ask for credit to the amount of £15.

From the information supplied to the department by defrauded firms, it appeared that no sooner had Mr. Smee Skeffington Smee taken up his residence at the Manor House than he had ordered watches, guns, opera-glasses, spirits, a costly billiard-table, and other goods, which he speedily converted into money, and in consequence of one of these transactions a warrant was granted for his arrest.

This warrant I held, but the difficulty was where to find Smee.

He was supposed to have travelled by train to London, and beyond this rumour I had no clue where to look for my man; but I returned to town on the assumption that he had sought refuge in the metropolis—the home of so many fugitives from justice. Men who commit crime in London generally run away from it; but they would frequently be safer to remain.

Most people have some habit, idiosyncrasy, craze, or hobby, and, luckily for the detective, criminals do not differ in that respect from ordinary mortals.

In the position in which I found myself I asked, " Had Smee any special fad or leaning?"

When clues are wanting it becomes a very important thing to obtain trustworthy information as to your man's particular weakness. I remember that one of my swindling prisoners had a great craze for cockatoos. He never saw a cockatoo advertised for sale without going after it. He did not keep the birds, however, but bartered them for something else

In that case I enticed the man to a particular place to inspect "a beautiful specimen," and he fell into the trap.

Now, as regards Smee, it is true that whilst inquiring about his habits I was given a description of him. But a man's description may be very misleading · so few people can describe a person with any degree of accuracy.

I recollect a lady swindler described to me by some people as a woman of twenty, and by others as a lady of thirty-five. When arrested she gave her age as seventeen, but those who had judged her older might have been nearer the mark, after all. The age of a lady is always uncertain.

On another occasion I remember looking for an individual who had been described to me as having lost a leg—but opinions differed whether the missing limb was the right or left—and he was cross-eyed.

It might be supposed that a one-legged, cross-eyed man could be easily picked out of a crowd The locality in which the suspected man resided was known, and an old colleague of mine stationed himself in the thoroughfare through which the man would probably pass.

"In three days," my colleague used to say, "I saw a dozen men who were cross-eyed and had each lost a leg, and not one of them was the man I wanted."

A man's habits are often a greater clue to his identification than his appearance.

In the course of inquiry I learned that Smee had been regularly in the habit of taking a leading weekly paper devoted to the interests of country gentlemen, and, in fact, he had left an unpaid bill for its supply to him. He had,

M

in the first instance, answered the advertisement of a Mr
Waite, a surveyor, who had let him the Manor House
furnished on a three months' agreement, without taking
much trouble about the references which Smee gave. One
of them was that of a banker at Y——.

Mr. Waite was able to tell me that Smee had formerly
lived at Maida Vale, in apartments.

I made inquiries at those lodgings, but the people knew
nothing of his then whereabouts.

The foregoing was the extent of my information, but
scanty though it may seem, it was sufficient to afford me
a clue.

I had remarked one point—Smee's great partiality for
the newspaper devoted to country gentlemen's sports and
pastimes.

I reasoned, too, on a theory which has more than once
proved correct, that a criminal is prone to return to his old
haunts, and therefore Smee would probably be found in the
neighbourhood of Maida Vale

My first step was to go to many of the firms who had
been defrauded, and ascertain of them that they had certainly advertised in the newspaper patronised by Smee, who
evidently had applied to them for goods in consequence.

Next I went to the office of the paper, and asked them
for a list of news-agents in Maida Vale and adjoining
districts who were likely to sell the publication in question,
telling them my object. One by one I visited the news-
agents, and finally discovered a shop which was then
supplying Smee with the paper, for he was meditating some
fresh fraud.

In that way I obtained his address, and proved the

correctness of my theory, for I arrested Smee within a very short distance of his old lodgings.

Smee served many months' imprisonment, and at the expiration of that term rejoined his wife and children. The wife had been the daughter of a yeoman, but Smee himself was of better position, his father having been in the merchant service and retired on a good sum of money which had been left to him.

His son, who was at that time twenty-five years of age, had induced him to take a large farm in the country, near to Y——, with a view to assisting in the management, but he spent his time with the young squires, and went swaggering about, neglecting his business, these dissipated habits soon having brought father and son to bankruptcy. Young Smee then, with his wife, came to Maida Vale, and afterwards embarked in the frauds for which I arrested him

When Smee came out of gaol he borrowed ten shillings from his brother, and with this capital began a new scheme of fraud—one of the cleverest which I have known It will be seen how he turned his knowledge of farming to account

With this capital of ten shillings he entered into negotiations for the purchase of an estate worth £31,000, and, what is more to the point, he nearly succeeded in buying it. The story I have now to tell is of the way in which his plans were frustrated.

The half-sovereign Smee laid out in headed note-paper, upon which he wrote to the agents concerned in the offering of the property mentioned for sale, and obtained from them "orders to view;" and as he was living near to the estate, it did not cost him much to make the journey thither.

Smee was a gentlemanly, smart fellow, but quiet. He

was not shrewd, but he would pass very well anywhere. His conversational powers were good, but he was careful never to talk much of himself.

Consequently, when Smee went to the estate and was introduced to the owner, he was not suspected; but I don't suppose that Smee would have succeeded so well in his preliminaries had the owner been a man of greater experience in the management of land. In fact, it was because of his want of knowledge on the point that he wished to dispose of the property.

Smee Skeffington Smee proved himself to be such a very pleasant fellow that Mr. B——, the owner of the estate, said to him that evening, " Where are you stopping, Mr. Smee ? "

" I shall go to the hotel at X—— if I can't get home to-night, which I wish to do, as I didn't bring my things with me."

" I trust that you will not run away, but remain here to-night," said Mr. B——, courteously—making a fatal mistake in thus offering hospitality to a stranger.

Smee, of course, accepted the invitation, remained in the house, and next morning, telling his host that he wished to write a letter, shut himself up in the library and took out some stamped paper—"Bolton Grange," which was the name of the estate.

He wrote to a large dealer in sheep, in the West of England, to the following effect :—

"Bolton Grange, April —, 18—.

" DEAR SIR,

" I have purchased this estate of Mr. B——, but find that the flocks have been very much impoverished.

It will be necessary to restock them, so shall be glad if you can send two hundred sheep (naming kind and price) to T—— Railway Station, to be delivered to my order on Tuesday next.

"Yours, etc.,
"Smee Skliffington Smel"

Smee took care to supply himself with enough letter paper from the case in the library to carry on the correspondence, and he made necessary arrangements for the delivery of letters to him which might come addressed to him at the Grange.

Well, it is on record that those two hundred sheep were actually delivered at T—— Station and handed over to a butcher who had some grazing land near to the railway, into which Smee had arranged they should be turned.

In a day or two, Smee wrote to the butcher, alleging that he no longer required the sheep, and was prepared to sell them at a loss.

The sheep were bought by the butcher and a cheque for £600 was sent to Smee, who immediately paid it to his credit at the bank at Y——, the town in which he and his father had formerly lived, drawing upon it very slightly for his immediate wants.

Having a balance at his bank, he next went to a money-lender and made representations to him which induced him to lend £500, and this £500 was also paid into the bank.

Smee was not a man of extravagant tastes and never drank, and he went about the whole scheme deliberately.

He was accustomed to go to and from Bolton Grange,

acting as an intending purchaser might do, never hurrying matters, but making certain suggestions, and finally agreeing to purchase the property for a certain sum.

It was arranged that £2500 should be paid as a deposit, and the deeds were then to be drawn up for the transfer of the title, etc.

Whilst these negotiations were in progress Smee wrote to another sheep-dealer, saying that as his place was understocked, he wished to buy eight hundred sheep, for which he would pay £1000 down, and the remainder in bills for short periods.

After some correspondence, the dealer agreed to supply the eight hundred sheep, and Smee sent his cheque for £1000 to Scotland.

At this stage of the affair it happened that Mr. B——— had a visitor staying with him at Bolton Grange, with whom he chatted about the approaching sale of property to Mr. Smee.

"M—— —" asked the visitor, who as it chanced, unfortunately for Smee, came from the very town in which Smee banked and where he and his father had originally lived, " do you say Smee?"

"Yes, Smee Skeffington Smee."

" And he banks at Y———?"

" Yes."

" The very same," cried the visitor. " My dear Mr B———, pray be cautious. Do you know this man? Is he in a position to pay you for Bolton Grange?"

"You alarm me, said Mr. B———, "you know something—you are concealing something. What am I to do?"

" If my suspicions are correct," answered the gentleman, " the best thing you can do is to write to Inspector Little-child, of Scotland Yard."

They wrote to me privately. I submitted the letter to the chief, and it became an official note

" Would you send me some of the gentleman's hand-writing?" I wrote in reply

They sent specimens, and I immediately recognized the handwriting as that of my old prisoner—Smee Skeffington Smee—the author of the Manor House frauds

I at once telegraphed the fact to Mr B——.

Steps were taken, and on the information of the West of England sheep-dealer a warrant was procured for Smee's arrest—not a moment too soon, for by this time the eight hundred sheep ordered in Scotland were placed on the rail. A " wire " stopped them *en route*.

But for the fortunate circumstance that the visitor at the Grange was from Y——, and was able to warn his host of Smee's true character the eight hundred sheep would have been delivered, and would no realized, probably, over £2000. This sum would have enabled him to pay the deposit asked for by the seller of the estate, and leave him with money in hand to supply his immediate wants

What Smee's ultimate object was I never knew, but amongst his papers I found correspondence which went to show that he had been actually negotiating for a mort-gage on the estate which had not then come into his possession.

It is a fortunate thing for the detective that a swindler, as a rule, preserves his correspondence.

Smee was arrested easily enough, and for the second

time came up for sentence, when the judge, in giving him a term of years, remarked—

"The ingenuity of the fraud perpetrated by the prisoner shows that he has in him the makings of a very dangerous criminal, especially as the offence must have been planned out in the seclusion of his cell whilst undergoing imprisonment on a former conviction, as he was no sooner liberated than he put his plans to execution.'

I fully agree with the judge, and I relate the story to indicate the lengths to which a man will go in committing fraud. Frauds, I have always found, present many extraordinary features not noticeable in other phases of crime, except, possibly, in some cases of forgery, or in murders which have required the exercise of considerable ingenuity to carry out.

CHAPTER XVII.

CAPTURES MADE AT SEA—THE STOWAWAY AND THE BOND STEALER

BOARDING a vessel to make an arrest has a peculiar interest to a detective, especially at night.

On one occasion I had to meet a ship in which a certain individual, who was "wanted" by the police, was supposed to be. It is not easy to identify persons in a crowd in such circumstances.

Certainly, an officer has generally the advantage of knowing a man's name, besides having been supplied with his description; and if he can contrive to board the vessel in sufficient time to get information before the passengers begin to disembark the matter is easy, and if, by mischance, the de--ve should fail, his prisoner may have luggage to pa-- --ough the Customs, which may aid the officer, should he miss him on board.

In this particular instance I had been waiting at the mouth of the Thames for three days, the vessel for which I was on the look-out having been detained by fogs in the Channel.

At last she hove in sight, and I lost no time in boarding her, eager to learn whether the man of whom I was in search was actually in the ship. I took myself at once

to the purser and made known to him my business The
passenger list was examined.   No name resembling the
one which had been supplied to me could be found

Presently the captain came into the purser's cabin   I
broke the matter to him, and he turned out a splendid
fellow, and put heart and soul into the affair.

All the stewards were called into the purser's cabin one
by one, but none of them could recognize the description
I gave as that of any passenger.

From the "information received"—upon which I was
acting—I couldn't tell whether my man would be a saloon,
intermediate, or steerage passenger, but we went through
the whole number without success.   I was quite resigned
to giving up the hunt as hopeless, concluding that some
mistake had been made by our informants on the other
side of the water.

Suddenly the captain, turning to the purser, exclaimed,
"What about that stowaway?   Doesn't he come near to
the description? '

"I don't think my man is likely to be a stowaway," said
I, "he has plenty of money."

"Oh!" cried the captain, "that's nothing to go by.
We have queer fish as stowaways at times."

"What sort of a man is the one you have on board just
now?" I asked with great interest.

"Well, he is a cut   what you would expect in a
stowaway.   In fact, when he was first brought to me, I
had a suspicion that some one would be waiting for him
when we reached this side "

"Where did he hide himself, captain?"

"He was found amongst the cattle fodder.   He certainly

must have induced some one on board to give him food until he was discovered; but although I questioned all the crew they each denied having seen him. I gave him a chance of paying his fare, but he said he couldn't. I now see why he preferred to do work instead he wanted to travel *incog.*"

By this time I was interested in the story of this stowaway, and accepted the captain's offer that he should be sent for, but nevertheless I had not much faith that he was the man I wanted.

Presently the stowaway was brought to the door of the purser's cabin, and, sure enough, if any reliance was to be placed in a description, there stood my man !

His characteristics had been cabled most correctly. There was no mistaking him, but his appearance was so irresistibly comic that I burst into laughter.

There was a look of wonderment and of scare upon his face, and his rig-out was the last which I should have expected him to wear. He was dressed as a sailor, and in his hand he held a large piece of cotton-waste, which he had been using in his work of cleaning brass, and in this employment he had succeeded in begriming himself most effectually.

"Halloa, Morison !   cried, using his real name, "what sort of a get-up do you call this ?"

My man seemed struck with the novelty of the situation —in fact, so much amazed was he that he entirely forgot to deny his identity, which rendered matters much easier for me, and we had more than one laugh together afterwards at his little ruse to get out of harm's way by posing as a stowaway.

I have had many adventures upon the waters of the
Thames when bent upon similar quests, but on each
occasion there was allowed me sufficient time for making
inquiries on board without putting the officers of the ship
to any inconvenience. Indeed, they were always ready to
give me any assistance; but it was otherwise when I had
to board a vessel at night at a port of call, at which a few
passengers were disembarked, and the ship then hurried on

In such disadvantageous circumstances I had once to
undertake a difficult case.

An extensive robbery of bonds had been committed in
New York   The full value of the stolen securities was
enormous, and the actual market value amounted to many
thousands of dollars

It happened that a certain man was suspected, and the
officers, under Chief Inspector Byrnes, had clearly established that the thief had quitted New York, but no clue to
his destination could be obtained by them at any of the
railroad depôts   As all outgoing vessels had been
" blocked" after the police had got to work, it was concluded that the man must be embarked upon a liner
bound for Hamburg, which had sailed immediately after
the perpetration of the robbery and before the loss of the
bonds had been reported to the police

A telegram, based upon this theory, reached London,
and was handed to me a few hours before the liner was
due at Southampton. I had barely time to catch the train
to that port and on arrival to board a tender which would
meet the steamer in Southampton Water.

We went down this arm of sea at night, and presently
discerned the lights of the German vessel bearing down

upon us. Speedily we were alongside, and her anchor dropped.

Unfortunately for me, dinner had just been finished, and many of the stewards were thus fully occupied. The purser was unapproachable, for he was up to his eyes in work, in conjunction with the agents of the company, and the officers were engaged in the various duties consequent upon the landing of passengers, specie, and mails.

No one was at leisure to listen to me, and all was noise, bustle, and confusion.

What was worse, I had only a description to guide me, and my difficulties can be better imagined than described when the task before me was to pick out, amidst these distracting circumstances and in a limited time—for the tender was ready to start—a particular man out of the several hundreds of passengers who were on board.

It was idle to expect much assistance from stewards, who were so much immersed in the necessary business of collecting luggage and "tips." At the most I could only put a question now and then, when a chance offered, and make the best of it. Yet, inwardly groaning, I realized that each single moment was precious, for the big liner was impatient to get under way again on her homeward journey.

At last a steward vaguely hinted that he thought a man answering to the description that I gave was about to land at Southampton.

I dare say it will be understood that in all these inquiries I had to be extremely cautious. I had spoken in whispers and in the most unconcerned way, fully realizing that one unguarded word or the least excitement might have betrayed my presence to the man of whom I was in search, for he, no doubt, would be listening with acute hearing to all that went on, and would be keeping his eyes open for any person who bore the smallest resemblance to a police officer

At last the moment came for the passengers who were to land at Southampton to be transferred to the tender My only and last resource was to watch the gangway, and one by one the people passed me, but I saw no person who corresponded to the details of the description.

But judge of my intense relief when almost the last man to make his appearance was an individual who answered to the description unmistakably. Several passengers who were proceeding to Hamburg shouted to him, " Good-bye, Bruce; good-bye," addressing him, however, by a name that I did not know, but as I did not expect that he would be running from justice under his own name, this fact did not alarm me.

A matter which concerned me much more was the thought—" Supposing that he denies that he is the man I want, and supposing he has packed the bonds into a parcel before leaving New York, and has mailed them to some *poste restante* on the Continent, or in London ? "

This plan he might very easily have adopted, with the intention of claiming the packet when the coast was clear, for the securities were bonds to bearer, easily convertible into cash.

It crossed my mind that it might be an awkward business to detain a man on the basis of a description only, without anything to confirm his identity, and the consequences might prove serious if, eventually, my prisoner turned out to be the wrong man

However, the man was of somewhat remarkable appearance. I verily believe that he had the yellowest hair I have ever seen.

So, having fully deliberated upon the situation, I quickly sat myself beside him upon the tender, with my back to him, and as we steamed towards Southampton I casually entered into conversation with another passenger on the other side of me

I waited until the journey up the Water was half completed, and the excitement of leaving the big ship had subsided Then I turned round and faced in the direction of the yellow-haired man, and resolved to try a ruse which, in similar circumstances, I have seldom known to fail

Quickly but tinctly, I called his real name—

" John ! '

He jumped ound as though I had struck him, and in the darkness of the night he peered into my face.

" Good evening, Mr. ——," I said, " welcome to England. I hope you have had a pleasant voyage."

" Yes," he replied, " but I don't know you. You have the advantage of me "

I perceived at once that he was prepared for a denial, for he was apparently recovering himself, but I taxed him direct—

" Why, you are Mr. ——, are you not ? Your name is John ——? "

' No," he replied , " it is not."

" Well," I said, " any other name will do equally as well, Mr. Bruce "—mentioning the name by which his fellow-passengers had addressed him

" Yes," he said, " that is my name."

"Just as you please," I continued, "but I am an officer of police, and I arrest you on the charge of stealing bonds in New York."

"You have made a mistake, sir," he retorted curtly, and in a nasty way.

"Very well," I said, "I must abide by the consequences, and as you are inclined to be quarrelsome, I will trouble you just to let me quietly put these handcuffs on I may tell you that if you do not accept the situation I have plenty of assistance on board this boat, and I shall have to handcuff you compulsorily"

I knew from previous cases that this threat would have the desired effect. My man could not stand the mention of handcuffs.

"Don't put them on," he begged of me. "Don't show me up before these people"

"Very well, then, I won't," I said; "only behave yourself and I shall treat you kindly."

It was not long before we were in friendly conversation, and by the time we had reached the Customs at Southampton I felt convinced that I had made no mistake in the arrest.

But my man was not going to resign his freedom so easily. His good temper, no doubt, was intended to hoodwink me. He knew the weakness of my chance of proving his identity.

His luggage was duly passed by the Custom House officers I searched his boxes for the bonds, but not one was to be found.

The thought recurred to me that he had taken the precaution to mail them, and at that possibility I was a little taken aback. I questioned him about the bonds.

"I never had them," he declared, "and haven't got them."

I searched his pockets as well as all his effects, but without lighting upon a trace of a bond, or any scrap of paper which pointed to his identity. I reflected for a few moments and the matter certainly appeared very awkward.

"Have you any other luggage, Mr. Bruce?" I asked.

"No," said he, but I fancied I perceived a sudden glance of dismay.

Then light dawned upon me.

By this time we had left the Customs shed, but I determined to go back, and accordingly we retraced our way

I saw the chief officer of Customs, and asked, "Is all the passengers' luggage cleared and claimed?"

"Yes," said he; "all but one trunk, which is unclaimed"

"I suspect that that trunk belongs to my prisoner," I said; "and I must try the lock"

"All right," he answered · ' go ahead."

With the keys I had taken from the prisoner I tried the lock, and to my delight one of them opened it

The Customs officer inspected the contents for me, but no bond was found.

No detective cares to be deprived of the chance of finding property that has been stolen, and as I was rather eager, for the recovery of the securities was of as much consequence as the arrest of the thief, I resolved to search for myself

I did so, turning over the contents of the trunk, but without result. Still I was not content. On a second examination I took up some linen shirts—quite clean.

N

Something impelled me to look into them, and it was well that I did so, for, lying flat inside the fronts of each, were some of the missing bonds

"What do you say to these?" I said, turning to the prisoner, who stood silently and sullenly by whilst watching the operation of unloading the shirts of their valuable linings

"Waal," he answered, "I guess it was your business to find the bonds, not mine."

CHAPTER XVIII.

MR BORROWDALE'S SAPPHIRE RING—HOW A MYSTERY WAS SOLVED.

THERE are burglars and burglars To me the ordinary type is uninteresting. He hangs about public-houses by day, and, like the bat, flies at night, and his methods of work are invariably the same Occasionally. when disturbed, he shows fight, and then he is often prepared to commit murder to avoid arrest.

But all burglars are not professional hands. I have known of bogus jobs, "put up" by small jewellers to avoid bankruptcy; and the first care that a police officer has, is to determine whether the thief is to be found within or without the premises.

Now to my story.

Mr. Borrowdale was a London banker who lived within the Metropolitan Police District in a lovely spot just beyond the smoke of the great city. A mysterious jewel robbery had taken place at his house, and I was sent down from Scotland Yard to make inquiries.

Woodbury Towers, Mr. Borrowdale's private residence, stood in its own grounds. Its gardens were beautifully laid out, and it was well supplied with tennis-lawns, dog-kennels, aviaries, and all the accessories of a well-maintained country house.

It was exactly the place which a ladder or portico thief would select for "putting-up" a job of the kind which we hear about so constantly in London. The robbery, usually of jewels, takes place at the dinner-hour, when all the servants are downstairs, and the bedrooms are left. Access is obtained by a dressing-room, where, perhaps in the wardrobe, the jewel-safe is, probably unlocked, the thieves using a rope or borrowed ladder to scale the portico. The bedroom doors are then screwed up, and whilst the thieves secure their booty, other members of the gang remain outside to give an alarm, to quiet the dog if necessary, and to hinder pursuit by stretching wires across the lawn to trip up pursuers.

The ladder thief by careful prospecting has invariably made sure that the booty is worth having, and the haul is, as a rule, a large one; but at Woodbury Towers the loss was comparatively small. The value of the stolen jewels was insignificant, but they included certain heirlooms and a certain sapphire ring.

The ring had, I gathered, been presented to a member of the family by a royal personage, and therefore it was treasured far above its intrinsic value. There were also missing a number of pins, rings, and brooches.

My first care was to look for the signs of a burglarious entry—the marks of a "jemmy," chisel, or other tool; but I found none.

Forming a theory that the burglary had not been committed from without, but from within, I cautiously questioned the servants in turn. The lady's-maid narrated the circumstances.

"The things must have been stolen between six and seven o'clock last evening," said the girl, breathlessly, "because I saw Mary, the housemaid, close all the windows in the bedrooms shortly before then. Soon after six I went into the young ladies' room and noticed several of the rings and things on the dressing-table."

"You are quite sure of that?"

"Oh yes, sir! And when I went in again, about half-past seven, they were gone."

"Why didn't you give an alarm, then?"

"Because I thought they were put away, sir."

The sapphire ring itself had been removed from a cabinet, in which it was contained in a secret drawer, and it was not until eleven o'clock at night that the robbery had been discovered.

In the course of this preliminary inquiry one or two points struck me which demanded explanation, but they yielded no clue.

Next I went to Mr. Borrowdale and asked him, "Has there been any previous robbery of jewellery at your house, sir?"

"Oh yes!" said he—"two months ago I had to discharge one of the men-servants. We suspected him of stealing a pin and a ring which I had given as a birthday present to my son."

"Can you tell me the whereabouts of this man at the present time?"

"I cannot. He had not long been with us, but perhaps one of the servants can assist you."

This they were unable to do.

I ran back to town, circulated my descriptions of the missing jewels in the usual channels, and then continued my investigation as to the character of each one of the servants; for suspicion naturally fell upon them.

I was so certain that I had not to look for the thief in the haunts of the professional burglar, that, unable to fix definitely the guilt upon the domestics, I began, acting upon a vague suspicion at first, to inquire about the members of Mr. Borrowdale's family.

With the housekeeper—a nice, elderly lady—I had frequent chats at Woodbury Towers

"Ah, yes!" said the dame, "I have been a very long time with the family. I nursed Master Frank—the eldest son, you know—upon my knee."

"Mr. Borrowdale is very particular in his habits?" I asked, following up a remark which the housekeeper had made whilst she had been recounting the doings of the whole household during the week preceding the burglary

"Yes, yes," she replied, "he likes to be methodical, and he is quite annoyed if all his family are not present at morning prayers. They are early, as he leaves for the City at nine, and he will not be hurried over breakfast."

"And are there family prayers at night?"

"Yes, and all the household attend them."

"Including Master Frank?"

"Not always. His father has been angry with him on that account. He frequently makes excuses for staying in town, long after banking hours. Once a fortnight he stays with some friends regularly."

CHIEF-INSPECTOR LITTLECHILD.

"Mr. Borrowdale is too particular a man to allow his son a latch-key, I imagine?"

"Oh yes! When Mr. Frank is late the butler sits up for him, and takes care that everything is properly fastened up for the night.'

"Mr. Frank was out late on the evening of the burglary, was he not?"

"Yes; he did not come home until after it was discovered —past eleven o'clock, but he was spending the evening with some friends in the neighbourhood, and he dined at home that day at seven."

I met Master Frank one night at the railway station, apparently by accident, but really by design; for I purposely went down by the train in which he usually travelled, and rubbed against him as we were passing the ticket collector, so that he could not help seeing me, upon which I bade him "Good evening."

The young fellow—he was about twenty-one—seemed quite pleased, and, as we walked towards his father's house, remarked, "Well, how are you getting on with your case?"

"Not very well, I am afraid I have positively no clue and nothing to work upon."

I watched his face narrowly, and perhaps only fancied I noted a gleam of satisfaction in his eyes.

Our conversation gradually drifted into talk about detective work, and the opportunities of seeing "life." I led the young fellow on to the subject of sacred concerts (he was rather shy of them), orchestral concerts, popular concerts, amateur theatricals, *matinées* at theatres, and the popularity of the present-day music-hall, taking these steps in easy gradation.

"Oh, I don't often get out," he said with a sigh; "the governor's so strict.   He does not like theatre-going, don't you know."

"Would you care to come with me one night, and take a turn round on the quiet?' I said.

"That I should, Mr. Littlechild," he answered. "You detective fellows see such a lot, and I don't care to go about with anybody in my own set—it might get to the governor's ears."

Accordingly, an appointment was made for the following Saturday, and we met on that evening at Scotland Yard.

My object in all this business was to learn Master Frank's particular tastes, and to discover, if possible, whether his salary or allowance was sufficient to gratify them.

We passed the Saturday evening very pleasantly and circumspectly. I was cautious that, should the outing come to Mr. Borrowdale's knowledge, no blame should attach to me for having led his son astray. Master Frank, if he had had any knowledge of the world, would have deemed me a "soft." A detective finds it convenient to assume that character sometimes.

Master Frank was quite content, however, with the milk-and-watery amusements in which we indulged. I think he would have regarded a visit to the British Museum as an act of dissipation that evening; and he spent his money in a niggardly way, apparently having to be careful of every shilling. He did not seem to be at all "flush;" and when we parted, it was with a feeling of compunction that I had been on the wrong scent, and had suspected in my heart a young fellow who was thoroughly well conducted, and who did not merit any reproach.

However, I had made sufficient progress with my new acquaintance to invite him out again, thinking that I owed him some amends. He accepted; and on another evening we met again.

I found Master Frank much less reserved. He was fond, I found, of a cigar, and a little later I treated him to liquor. He had more than one glass of whisky, and then his tongue loosened, and he confided to me that his father was stingy, and kept him upon a very short allowance.

"It doesn't matter," said I, and continued to "stand treat;" but as my companion warmed to the enjoyment of the evening, he began to spend his own cash so freely that I wondered at his remark that his pocket-money was deficient, for he appeared to have plenty.

Young Borrowdale soon displayed a much more familiar acquaintance with the music-halls where ballets are performed than I had given him credit for, and he took me to several first-class bars. He was evidently well known to the barmaids, and one of them said—

"Well, Frank, you have been quite a stranger lately."

"Halloa," I thought, "a barmaid does not address a customer by his Christian name for nothing."

I still remained on my guard, and pretended neither to hear nor to see what was going on; and Frank, having taken more drink than was good for him, parted with me that night on the jolliest terms possible.

On the following day I strolled to the West End, and dropped into the bars which Frank and I had visited on the preceding night, and chatted pleasantly with the young ladies, leading the conversation to the subject of my companion.

"Gay young spark," exclaimed one of them, "but he's a good-hearted chap, he brings us such nice flowers."

The barmaid who had called Borrowdale "Frank" approached, and I bantered her a little about it, which soon put her on good terms. She was a very good and sensible girl.

"I am afraid," she said, "Frankie is too good-natured. A lot of people will be sure to fasten upon him."

"Yes," said I, "he is a kind-hearted fellow, and never seems happier than when he is making a present.'

"That is quite true," she replied. "He gave me this ring"—showing me her finger.

"Is that so?" I said. "It looks very pretty. What is that stone? I have never seen one like it before. Is it a blue diamond? It certainly isn't glass."

"Glass!" she echoed, tossing her head. "I should think not, indeed! It is a sapphire, and I am told that it is very valuable."

"It certainly is very pretty," I rejoined. "Would you mind my looking at it?"

"Oh no," and she took the ring off and handed it to me.

I carefully examined the ring, and then returned it to her. Turning my back to the bar, I took out my printed list, and there, plainly enough, was the description of the sapphire ring, identical in all respects with the one which the barmaid said Frank Borrowdale had given to her.

"Young lady," I said in a low voice to the barmaid, "I am Inspector Littlechild, of Scotland Yard. Just read that description of a stolen sapphire ring, and tell me if it does not correspond with yours."

The girl grew very frightened, but I assured her that she had nothing to fear, and no mention would be made to her employer of the matter, but she must allow me to take the ring back to its proper owner.

She consented, and the missing sapphire ring was placed in my possession

My duty now was clear. However painful the task which devolved upon me, I had to tell the father that his son — he was about to become a partner in the bank—was a thief.

That evening I went once more to Woodbury Towers. Father and son were both at home, and in an hour they would be dressing for dinner. Now was my time.

I first saw Mr. Borrowdale in his study, and told him as gently as I could what I had discovered.

"But," he cried, with an agonized face—like a drowning man catching at a straw—"his mother might have given him the ring"

I knew, and he knew, that in his despair he was trying to deceive himself.

At last he broke a painful silence by asking—

"What do you propose to do, Mr. Littlechild?"

I thereupon suggested that the youth of his son was in itself some apology, and that he would never forget the lesson. I hinted that the young fellow should be called into the room, confronted with the evidence of his guilt, and if he showed contrition, and divulged what had become of the remainder of the stolen property, that I could withdraw from the inquiry.

Mr. Borrowdale sat back in his armchair, grave and dejected, thanked me for my consideration, and rang the bell.

A footman answered the summons.

"Tell Mr. Frank Borrowdale," said the heart-broken father in a voice over which he had lost control, "that I wish to see him here immediately."

The servant withdrew, and in a minute or two the prodigal son entered the study. He was not aware of my presence in the house, and when he saw me, and glanced at his father's grave face, he perceived that something had happened. His gay and jaunty manner changed to one of apprehension and alarm.

The father motioned me to speak.

"Mr. Frank Borrowdale," I then said, "I have strong evidence in my possession that the jewellery which your father has missed was stolen by you."

"Sir!" he cried, stepping angrily towards me, "how dare you——"

When his father interposed, and cried—

"Stop! Don't add lying to your thieving, sir!"

At that moment, with an exhausted look, he made a movement towards my hand, in which I held the ring

I held up the jewel to the young man, and said—

"Do you recognize this?"

He glared as though he had seen an apparition, and then, rushing to his father, he fell upon his knees, and, with bitter sobs, implored forgiveness.

Placing the ring upon the table, I said to Mr. Borrowdale—

"You have no further need of me?"

He bowed his head; and I left father and son together.

CHAPTER XIX.

A FRAUD UPON FREEMASONS, AND HOW IT GAVE MY CLUE.

IN criminal detection there are often great disappoint ments, with certain consolations, as the following narrative will show.

A man of gentlemanly appearance took furnished lodgings at a highly respectable house in the West End. He called himself Lieutenant-Colonel Teviotdale.

In a day or two he presented himself at a well-known jeweller's in the neighbourhood, and purchased a piece of jewellery. A few days later he gave an order for more— of the value of nearly £1000 The articles, he explained, were intended as wedding presents to a friend—a lady. She lived, he said, in the country.

Lieutenant-Colonel Teviotdale was very particular about this order, and extremely fussy with regard to the description of case in which the articles—a pair of diamond earrings and brooch—should be put. No case which the jeweller had in stock would suit his taste.

"I will supply a case myself," he said finally, and accordingly he did so, and requested that the jewellery should be sent to his address.

The diamond ear-rings and brooch were duly fitted into the velvet case, and, at the time appointed by the apparently well-to-do colonel, were taken by the jeweller himself to his house; but, as he did not know his customer, he deemed it prudent to ask an assistant to accompany him.

They were ushered into the room, and were received by Colonel Teviotdale with well-bred courtesy.

He inspected the sparkling jewels, and expressed his complete satisfaction with them.

"I will,' said he, " wrap the case in brown paper, seal it, and direct it, so that there shall be no mistake, and I will then ask you to forward it immediately you have cleared my cheque I am sorry I cannot pay you in notes, but I do not like to keep so much money in the house."

"Quite so," said the jeweller, blandly; "it would be tempting burglars."

Colonel Teviotdale took up the case, and turned to a side table. There was a sheet of brown paper upon it, and nothing more. Then he carefully wrapped the parcel up, sealed it, and addressed it to "Lady M——, Belleisle Castle, Notts," and immediately handed the package to the jeweller. Producing a cheque-book from a drawer, he wrote out and signed a cheque for the amount, and handed it to the jeweller, who took it with many thanks on his part, and extreme inward satisfaction at the prompt settlement which had been arrived at.

Colonel Teviotdale remained at his lodgings, whither in the course of the evening other tradesmen came with valuable goods; and each one departed with " a little cheque," as Mr. Irving, as " Digby Grant," used to say in Albery's *Two Roses*.

No one questioned the *bona fides* of the transactions

That night a four-wheeled cab left the colonel's chambers, on its roof were parcels and packages innumerable, and the very respectable house in the West End knew the gallant officer no more

In due course the jeweller paid the cheque which he had received in payment for the diamond ear-rings, etc., into his bank; but in a few hours a messenger brought it back to him, saying that the cheque was a forgery.

"A forgery! Well, it is fortunate that I had not despatched the jewels, and there will be no great loss," the tradesman cried.

The jeweller took the parcel, unpacked it, and opened the case. No diamonds glittered in the box, except those of the Derby Bright or Wallsend description In a word, the case contained coals!

The case was the exact counterpart of the one in which the jewels had been originally placed; and it was clear now that Colonel Teviotdale, when he turned to the side table to wrap the parcel up, had adroitly "rung the changes" by substituting one parcel for the other, and sealed up the coals instead of the diamonds.

Of course, it turned out that the cheques given to the other tradesmen were equally worthless.

At the outset the inquiry, which was duly placed in the hands of Scotland Yard, was not mine; but " from information received," as the technical phrase goes, I was privately put into possession of some sort of a clue, and I took the case up.

The whereabouts of the bogus colonel were entirely unknown.   Even his identity at that stage was unsuspected.
He had simply disappeared with his spoil—diamonds,
expensive costumes, ladies' trousseaux, sealskin mantles,
overland trunks, and other goods which he had obtained
from tradesmen.   One firm alone had been victimized to
the extent of £200

We had the forged cheques to guide us, but they did
not amount to much, until, as I have said, a little bird
whispered to me that the man to whom the cheque-book
had been originally issued was still living and not to be
found.   Up to that moment my colleagues had learned
that the cheque-book was supplied to a person who had
been originally in business in the East End, but had gone
out of it some years since, and no one knew whither he
had betaken himself

The question which now suggested itself was very
naturally—To whom did this retired tradesman part with
his cheque-book, and for what purpose?

It might be thought that this part was easily to be
answered by putting the question direct to the man himself; but a detective has often to adopt a roundabout
course, and in this case a direct interrogation was not
possible, for it was conceivable that the owner of the
cheque-book was himself a party to the frauds.   True,
there were no signs that he had been, for he was not
"flush" of money, and everything pointed to the supposition that this individual had been duped.

In his early experience he had been pretty well fleeced
by members of the "crooked" gang, who sold to him
"duffing" jewellery—that is, goods apparently of solid

gold, but plated only, sufficiently deep, however, to with-stand the acid test. The rogues had ruined him, and at length had thrown him on one side as of no further use

" Honour among thieves," it is said; but I confess I never saw much of it

It was not difficult to trace this man, but the real problem was in what manner to approach him. To go straight to one of his class for information would be as fruitless a task as to enter a bank, present a forged cheque, tell the clerk that it was forged, and then expect to have it cashed

What resource was open to me? Obviously, as I could not speak to the retired tradesman myself, I should have to get some one else to " draw him."

Now, as my knowledge of this man increased, I found that among his acquaintances there was a certain person to whom a colleague of my own had once done a very good turn.

Gratitude exists among the " crooks," and frequently a detective, in return for some act of kindness, will receive information from them which money cannot buy.

My colleague, at my request, interviewed the man he had befriended, and soon found that he could rely upon his sense of gratitude. We had no occasion to tell this individual why we wished to learn what had become of the cheque-book, and we instructed him first to " pump " the retired tradesman on the subject, and, if he did not respond to cajolery, then to hint darkly that he was going to be " tapped "—i.e. taken into custody on charges connected with the forged cheques—and that his probable arrest was being talked of by some of the " crowd."

As we had surmised, the latter alternative, which played

o

upon the retired tradesman's fears, was successful, for he had never been in gaol, and he blurted out—

"I know nothing about the cheques. All I can tell you is that a chap from America, who had just come, seeing them among my papers, asked me for them, and I let them go, as they were of no use to me."

So far good! But who was the "chap from America"? And where was he?

These questions would have been very indiscreet to ask, and they were not put; but I had to find out all the same. Slowly and cautiously I went to work, ferreting here and there, gleaning odd scraps of information, but never hitting upon the name and address of the "chap from America."

One item interested me. I chanced to overhear from people who were cognizant of the fact that when this man came from the States he was very hard up, and, as a Freemason, had received a sum of £5 from the benevolent fund of a certain lodge.

"Strange," I thought; "this smacks very much of fraud."

I communicated to the secretary of the fund my suspicions that the man he had aided was a dangerous thief.

Whatever the secrecy Freemasonry imposes, the secretary thought it his duty to help me. "But," said he, "what is the man's name?"

This was precisely what I wished to know myself, but I knew of no name except that of Colonel Teviotdale and other assumed ones.

"I am afraid that I can't assist you, then," said the secretary, "unless, perhaps, you can give the date."

Again I was nonplused, but, at my wits' end, I said, " Would it help you at all to recollect the incident if I told you that it is possible that the man made some allusion to his having been in America ? "

" Ha ! " he exclaimed. " I believe we did do something for a man some time ago who had just returned from the States, but I can't recall the date."

I begged that he would go through his books, and he consented. It was a tedious task, and as he plodded from A onward my hopes declined and, when we got to W, I began to regard the matter as hopeless, when suddenly he exclaimed—

" This looks something like the case—Lieutenant N., United States Navy, referred by XX., residing at X. Street."

I eagerly noted the address, thanked the official, and in a minute or two I was being whirled to Hoxton in a cab, to reconnoitre the neighbourhood in which X. Street is situated.

A little girl left the house in X. Street for some milk, and with her I entered into conversation, and learned from her that Mr. N. had lived in the street some weeks before, at her mother's house. The mother proved to be a very respectable person, and I had no trouble in making open inquiry of her.

" Oh yes," said she, " Mr. N. occupied furnished apartments here with Mrs. N., as she called herself. They were queer people, and I was glad to get rid of them. I don't think they were honest folk. Such lovely things used to be sent to them. One night an outfit came—fit for a princess, sir. Mrs. N. showed me the things. There were magnificent dresses and a real sealskin jacket. And her husband, sir, his jewellery was the solidest you ever see—most expensive, I'll be bound. I was given to understand they had lived in America, where Mr. N. had 'made his pile,' as he used to say affable-like."

"You don't happen to know where they have gone?"

"No, sir, I don't, and that's the truth; but it can't be very far away, sir. My little boy saw the woman near the Angel a week ago, dressed grandly."

"Did Mrs. N. wear the dresses you have described?"

"Yes; she had some altered. Miss Jones—that's the dressmaker, sir—told me she altered a splendid dinner gown into a walking dress for her, and it was a dreadful shame"

"Was that since they left you?"

"Yes, sir."

"Where does Miss Jones live?" I asked, repressing my eagerness, for the scent was growing warm.

"In B. Street, sir, No. 7, pull the top handle, and knock twice. By the way, sir, a funny thing happened while they were here. My little boy—Johnny, come here, sir!—that's the little chap, sir, he's a sharp lad, and passed his standards, sir. Well, as I was a-saying, my little boy and me was walking in Upper Street, and passed the police-station, which perhaps you know, sir, when all of a sudden he stopped me and cried, 'Isn't that like Mr. N., mother?' I looks up, and there on the wall, enough to knock me down, sir, was the picture of my lodger, a really striking likeness, sir, with something written about a robbery in Hatton Garden; but, of course, it was only a coin—cidence."

"Just so," said I.

The information was really startling, and it confirmed the suspicion that I had already formed that the man for whom we were searching was the notorious M., *alias* V., whose photograph was published on the reward bills concerning the Hatton Garden diamond robbery, which he was supposed to have planned, and in which it was believed he took a leading part.

The chase became exciting.

I called next on the dressmaker, asked as a matter of business for Mr. N.'s address, and she gave it to me without ado.

I went to the street at once, carefully and cautiously took its bearings, and discovered that in the window of the house in which N   as lodging there was a small card, "Apartments to Let

Next morning I took counsel with my colleagues, and we decided to put a "commercial traveller" into the vacant rooms. Accordingly we selected an officer, arranged references (if required), including the best kind of reference, rent in advance, and instructed him to take whatever rooms there might be to let.

We rigged out our young friend with samples, and, taking his luggage, he entered into occupation of a front bed and sitting room.

By this time we were aware that our man, Mr. N., *alias* Colonel Teviotdale—as we believed—was on the Continent, where, it was said, he was engaged with others in some big job. We were able to ascertain this information directly we knew that Mr. N. was the notorious M.

Our "commercial traveller" had been expressly instructed to keep his ears and eyes open, and his mouth shut, and it was arranged that should Mr. N. arrive home during the night our assistant's blind should be turned a certain way in the morning.

We took care to keep our spy well supplied with correspondence, so that he should be compelled to spend some time in the house answering the letters, but he went out daily with his samples, and was regular in his habits.

Morning after morning my colleague and I were outside the house, but there was no signal.

Our officer in the house got upon good terms with the landlady, and one day in chatting with him she told him that she had another gentleman lodger, and that he was abroad, but she added, " His wife expects him by the night mail any night."

But it chanced, after all, that our hopes were dashed to the ground.

One night the news was flashed by wire from Brussels that a gang of English thieves had been arrested, and, to my bitter disappointment, the name of our man—the man we had hoped to make a prisoner—was among them.

Having thus lost the salmon, we had to be content with the trout. We went at once and arrested the woman, and secured a large quantity of property.

M., *alias* V., *alias* Lieutenant N., *alias* Colonel Teviotdale, spent a term of years in a Continental prison, and on his return to London was arrested, and on the charges then preferred against him he is now undergoing ten years' penal servitude.

As to his antecedents, for some years he had confined his crimes to forgeries upon the Post Office and the theft of mail-bags. He was several times convicted—once for twenty years—and it was when he was liberated on ticket-of-leave from this sentence that he went to America, having failed to report himself as required.   While in the States he obtained possession of the papers and property of Lieutenant N., of the United States Navy, and thus he passed himself off as a Freemason, and obtained the £5 from the benevolent fund which gave me my important clue to his identity, if not to his arrest.

CHAPTER XX.

WHY MEN HAVE "GONE WRONG"—SOME CRIMES TRACED TO THEIR ORIGIN.

"A MAN overboard!"

It was too true! A moment before, the man who was now in the trough of the sea had been my prisoner, handcuffed, and just about to be landed at Queenstown.

How it happened I cannot exactly tell. A colleague was in front of the man, and I was behind him; but he rolled between the two of us, fell into the water, and sank at once, like a stone.

I leaped over the bulwarks by the side of the paddle box, and at the same moment a sailor jumped into the churning of the sea, at the risk of losing his life, for the water was so cold that he could scarcely grasp the rope which I threw to him. It seemed that two lives would be lost.

At last our prisoner rose to the surface on his back, and he lay upon the waves with his hands secured. He was helpless, unable to move a finger.

"For Heaven's sake, save me, Mr. Littlechild!" he gasped

By this time a boat had been lowered, and, in its eager

rush to the place where the man was making this agonizing appeal, it ran over him, knocking him almost senseless.

But at last, amid much excitement in the wintry morn, he was pulled on board; and, as we were now alongside the pier, he was entrusted to our charge, and we lost no time in carrying him to the nearest police-station in a jaunting car. I peeled his clothes off in a cell—the poor wretch was shaking with ague—and I rolled him in blankets, and laid him in front of a fire

Two hours afterwards—so close is comedy to tragedy in real life—I found him comfortably recovered, telling the Irish policemen yarns, and making them roar with laughter.

Curiously enough, the same man nearly committed suicide whilst at Cork, which makes me think that his fall into the sea was intentional.

Some time later he was, in London, committed to prison, and I went to the gaol with the object of warning the chief warder that the man had a fancy to take his own life. I missed him from the ranks of men in the exercise-yard, and inquired where he was.

"Well, it's rather strange you should ask," replied the chief warder, "for he has just tried to cut his own throat with a knife which he was permitted to use at meal-times."

I have recalled this man's case because it bears upon a question which has often been asked—"Does not familiarity with crime in itself lead to men becoming criminals?" In a word, does not the detective run the risk of becoming the man who is "wanted" by the police?

This man, who three times made a determined attempt to end his existence, had had a singular career He was originally a prison warder, and whilst acting in that capacity a notorious swindler came under his charge.

The prisoner induced his custodian to break the regulations by bringing tobacco and messages into the gaol from his friends outside. This breach of discipline was discovered, and the warder was discharged.

Then, the swindler having been released, the ex-warder was met by this dangerous friend, who said—

"Out of a crib, eh? That comes of being honest. Well, I never desert a pal, and I'll find you something to do— merely fetch letters, and do odd correspondence. It is quite straight."

The ex-warder gladly accepted, and, step by step, he embarked upon a career of crime: first as a subordinate, and then on his own account, until, finally, he was frequently in prison, and was known to me as an accomplished swindler.

So, in this instance, at all events, one can trace the evil results of bad company upon a man who is "down on his luck," but, nevertheless, there have been very few policemen who have "gone wrong"

I have frequently made it a point to endeavour to learn from criminals how they came to drift into crime; but it is seldom that I have been able to get to the actual facts, and the real state of the case has nearly always been a matter of conjecture. But I am constrained to the belief that bad associations, especially in youth, lead to boys becoming criminals. I join, too, in the protest against pernicious literature as a fruitful cause of crime.

"How came you to be a criminal?" I asked an old convict once. This man had spent nearly a quarter of a century in prison.

"Oh,' he replied, "I was allowed to do as I liked when a boy, and loafed about with a lot of street lads. They used to make me keep a look-out for them whilst they went into small shops and stole goods, or sneaked the till, but I was not a thief myself at that time. I was put into a situation, and had to run errands for men in a workshop, and had to fetch beer. It occurred to me that I might make some pocket-money by getting cheaper beer than was ordered, and charging the men full price for it. I made in this way a penny on the pot; also a halfpenny on a rasher of bacon. At last I was discovered, and didn't I catch it all round ! I was kicked out, and left to shift for myself.

"I lodged in a common doss-house, where I fell in with counterfeiters, who engaged me in their 'snide' (false money) business. I was induced to pass bad money, and soon 'fell' (was arrested). I never tried to get straight again, and when at liberty I turned to a bit of burglary, and thieving generally."

I have noticed during my career that most notorious criminals come from the land of Stars and Stripes, for in America precocity is directly encouraged, and precocity in a boy is apt to drive him into paths of crime.

One of the most dangerous men I have ever known was accustomed to live in London in great style, and was absent from his home only on those occasions when some great "job" was on hand. At intervals this man netted vast sums · probably, no living criminal has been more successful, financially, than he.

This rogue, during his leisure, lived like a gentleman, occupying a surburban house, which stood in his own grounds, with stables and all conveniences. But the owner was cautious in one matter. No strange servant was ever allowed to enter the establishment. He surrounded himself with faithful allies, who were perfectly mute as to the proceedings which went on within the garden walls.

In this security, passing as a gentleman of means, false keys, and all necessary burglar's implements, might be manufactured, plans matured, and conferences held, without a soul being the wiser. The robberies were generally committed on the Continent, and the "swag" generally consisted of diamonds, bonds, or bullion.

'Why did not the police detect him?" it may be asked

The plain answer to this pertinent question is, that it is out of the question constantly to watch a man whose "jobs" are done at long intervals—months, or even a year or two elapsing between them.

Moreover, the man was able to put pursuit at defiance, as he kept his own yacht, like Wells of Monte Carlo, with a crew of twenty He was here or there, as the fit pleased him.

Again, he was so cunning that in the case of nearly every job in which he was engaged, it was so skilfully planned that very little evidence could be adduced against the prime mover, and he did not scruple to get the better of his confederates.

I want to make it clear that I am not picturing a gentleman burglar from imagination. This man lives, but he is now in prison on the Continent. The story of his last "fall" is interesting

The robbery in which he was concerned was a single-handed business. He had run short of funds, and it is my impression that none of his old confederates would help him

His object was to discover the method of handling the parcels of bonds and securities conveyed in the Continental mail from London, and he instituted a close observation at a Belgian railway-station of some importance.

He noticed that small parcels on arrival were placed in a box under the seat of the driver of the van. The box was always padlocked. Following the van on its round, he noted where the parcels were delivered.

Taking advantage of the driver's absence, he carefully observed the shape of the padlock, and his next move was to obtain another padlock to resemble it as closely as possible.

Then he purchased a blouse and cap, such as are commonly worn by Belgian carmen, and, having selected from his " armoury " a small jemmy, he once more followed the van.

Waiting for his opportunity, it presently came.

The driver got off his seat to deliver a parcel, and my expert friend immediately jumped into the man's place and drove rapidly away.

A convenient distance having been placed between the thief and the driver of the van, the former lost no time in breaking off the padlock, and abstracting the valuables from the box under the seat. His intention was to substitute the other padlock for the broken one, and then to leave the van by the wayside; but his movements had been observed by some workmen, who, meeting the driver of the van in full cry, told him of the thief's whereabouts. The driver renewed his pursuit, and succeeded in catching the rogue red-handed.

It was for this little escapade that this prince of burglars is now incarcerated in a foreign prison

There was one strange coincidence in connection with this arrest.

One of this man's colleagues, having found himself in possession of funds, retired to the German States, and purchased a castle and a title. Henceforward he was known as the Baron, and he lived the life of a landed proprietor, severing himself from his old associates

But money gave out, and the Baron was under the necessity of replenishing his depleted exchequer by the proceeds of another haul

The contemplated matter in question was the robbery of a bank in a certain Belgian town, the very one in which the prince of burglars a little later was engaged in prospecting in the manner that I have described

Unluckily for the Baron, the bank robbery failed, and, still more unfortunately for him, he drew a revolver upon the officer who arrested him.

The Baron looked to his chief, the owner of the yacht, to act as a good friend to his wife during his incarceration; but he shirked that duty, and one day, in his cell, the Baron fervently exclaimed—

"Would that the Boss" (as he called him) "were here!"

To his utter bewilderment the wish of the Baron was fulfilled to the letter; for, when the robbery of the mail van led to the capture of the "Boss," this man was actually taken to the prison in which his confederate was confined.

It is not unprofitable to recall one or two facts in the boyish history of this daring burglar, in proof of my contention that precocity in children is a thing greatly to be dreaded.

Little Abel, as I may call him, was, in his schooldays (an intimate friend of his once told me), a very precocious child, addicted very much to "trading" with his companions in playthings, to their disadvantage.

He stated himself that he learned this lesson by the example of a much older boy, who, when Abel was only six years of age, offered him a brand-new penny for two old ones. The bright new copper penny seemed so very much like gold to little Abel that he gladly made the exchange, and when he arrived home he proudly showed his prize to his father, saying—

"See, dad, I've got the better of another boy by giving him two old pennies for this new one."

However, the father took a different view of the transaction from that which little Abel's finance had led him to form; and, moreover, he gave his son such a sound whipping that the boy never forgot the moral: "Get the best of your neighbour in every way you can, and take care he does not get the best of you"

"From that day," relates a friend of Abel's to me, "no one, friend or foe, honest man or crooked man, nigger or Indian, relatives or strangers, white man or black, ever got the better of Abel, and, until his recent 'fall,' he has not served more than two years and a half in prison, which fact alone places him as the most successful burglar of the present time."

As an example of the unscrupulous character of this man Abel, upon the same authority I may tell the story of the manner in which he got the better of a confederate in the theft of the celebrated Gainsborough picture from a private gallery in Bond Street.

This burglary, it will be remembered, excited a great stir at the time. All the newspapers contained accounts of the mysterious disappearance of this valuable canvas; and I dare say the following revelations will be news to a great many people who are still interested in the subject and are at a loss to understand how the theft could have been committed.

It was done in this manner—

Abel and a second man were engaged in the job. The former clambered upon the shoulders of his confederate, and, by the aid of awning stays, pulled himself to the level of the second-story windows, hiding himself behind a large sign-board, until the policeman on his beat in the early morning plodded by.

When the coast was clear all that remained to be done was to unfasten the window-catch with an instrument which had been specially made for the purpose. Then the thief raised the sash, slipped into the picture gallery, cut out the painting carefully from its frame, rolled it up, and passed it out of the window to his colleague in the street.

He followed the picture in person, closing the window after him, and leaving no clue.

" But how did Abel get the better of the transaction ? "

" Well," said my informant in answer to this question, " he pretended to his confederate that he had sold the Gainsborough picture for a mere bagatelle—it was worth £5000—and he persuaded his partner to accept £50 as his share of the haul, when at that very time the painting had never passed out of Abel's hands; and I believe it is to this day under his control."

CHAPTER XXI.

A SUPERSTITIOUS CRIMINAL—"UNHAPPY RETURNS OF THE DAY."

IT happened that a certain individual was "wanted" in France, on a charge of embezzlement. As in most extradition cases, the necessary documents were sent to Scotland Yard by the French police purely "on spec." It was supposed that he must have come to London, and that was all; but in the ordinary course, to be prepared for anything which might arise, a provisional warrant was obtained.

The particulars supplied by the French authorities were very meagre. They gave a description of the accused, it was true, but no other means of identifying him. Curiously enough, however, although they were, apparently, unable to forward a photograph of the man, they did append to the *dossier*, or docket, a likeness of his wife. It was the portrait of a very handsome woman.

Most important of all, as the sequel showed, the correct name of the criminal was given. It was a singular one— François Tascheritz.

Perhaps it cannot be conceived that a man who had committed fraud under this name should have believed

P

himself secure in a neighbouring country whilst he still retained it.   However, this lapse of ordinary precaution was just one of those things which mar the plans of the dangerous classes, and give the police their opportunity or clue.   Besides, I have noticed that though a man does not himself mind taking a false name, there always seems a reluctance on his part to ask his wife to do so too, she having had no share in his crime.

At all events I was reading a Sunday newspaper when my eye fell upon a police case, in which the name of Madame Tascheritz figured as the prosecutrix.   She had charged her domestic servant with stealing a bottle of brandy, and the prisoner had been remanded for a week.

It occurred to me that it would be worth the inquiry whom this Madame Tascheritz might be.   I took out the photograph of the wife of the man for whose arrest I held the warrant, and resolved to attend the police-court when the servant girl would be before the magistrate on remand.

I soon ascertained that the prosecutrix had not put in an appearance, and, much to my vexation, no one could give me a description of her husband.   The constable who had the case in hand had merely seen "Madame Tascheritz" on the night when she preferred the charge, and had taken such little notice of her that he was unable to identify the photograph.

Not knowing how far the girl might be handled with safety, I obtained access to the cell in which she was awaiting her turn to take her place in the dock, and allowed her to imagine that I was a solicitor.   It is by no means unusual for certain legal practitioners to pick up their clients in a similar way; and hence it was not difficult to get into conversation. I talked her kindly about her case, and, finally, having felt m v, told her that I wanted her to assist me in my research.

I asked the girl what Monsieur Tascheritz was like, and as soon as I thought I could trust her, I ventured to show her the portrait of the woman which I had in my possession.

"Oh !" she exclaimed. "That's missus !"

So here, at last, was the merest clue to work upon.

Madame Tascheritz, for some reason—perhaps it was a foreboding of disaster—did not come to the police-court.

"I think I can get you off, and I shall expect you to help me," I said to the prisoner.

As no prosecutor had appeared, a private explanation to the magistrate sufficed, for he at once perceived that the interests of justice might be served by the immediate discharge of the girl, rather than that a further remand should be taken. So the servant was liberated.

Of course she was able to confirm the address of Madame Tascheritz given in the charge sheet, and I began to keep patient observation upon the house occupied by the Tascheritz family.

They lived in good style, had three or four servants, and passed as highly respectable folk, on terms of intimacy with many professional people. I gathered that Monsieur Tascheritz had some connection with the musical world, and acted as agent to operatic artistes In the exercise of his duties in making engagements he would frequently have to leave home suddenly on hurried journeys to the Continent and elsewhere. In fact, he travelled very much, and came home rarely—on which occasions he would remain at his West End residence for a night, and then be off again.

It was a difficult thing to "locate" him; and my task was made doubly difficult by the extraordinary fact that a friend of the Tascheritz family, who was frequently at the house, resembled the man I wanted in a remarkable degree. This circumstance rendered the whole most extremely complicated, perplexing, and even dangerous, for to have arrested the wrong man would have been a fatal mistake.

For a long while we watched and waited—a very tedious business at the best of times.

At length I was satisfied that the right Mr. Tascheritz had come home. I had the servant placed in a favourable position to see him unobserved, and she confirmed my view by exclaiming, "That is the man."

So I arrested him, and he was taken to the police-station.

And now comes the most singular part of the whole story.

Whilst Monsieur Tascheritz was being detained at the police-station he sent for me to his cell.

"Have I your permission to write a letter?"

"Yes," I replied. "You may do so; but I must see what the letter contains"

"Certainly," he replied, "if that is usual."

He then wrote—I recollect the words perfectly—

"My darling wife,—Remember it is the 19th of May. I am arrested. Come and see me."

And that was all he wrote.

I read these few lines, and said, "Yes, that is all right; but I don't quite understand one part of it: 'Remember it is the 19th of May;' there seems to be some mystery about that. What is the meaning of it?"

A shadow passed over the man's face, and he answered quietly—

"She will know what it means. It is really nothing."

"But," I persisted, "there must be something in it, and I should like to know."

"It is nothing, it is nothing," he repeated in a tone as though he were trying to convince himself of the truth of the words. "It is a foolish matter—very foolish—child's play."

My curiosity was aroused, and as I still held to the point the prisoner said at length, "Well, I will tell you"

Then he told this strange story; for this tale is no flight of fiction, but strictly true.

"In my part of the country," said he, "in the village where I was born, the people are very superstitious. There was an old dame—a 'wise woman' in the district—to whom the parents were accustomed to take their children in order that their fortunes might be told. When quite a little boy I was carried to her cottage, and she, with many mystic ceremonies and rites, began to unravel my destiny— to tell my fortune, as you say."

"I hope she prophesied good luck?" I said.

"Not so. It is not necessary that I should repeat all the fortune-teller said. The portion which concerns me now included these words. 'Be careful,' said she, impressively, 'be very careful on your thirtieth birthday, for evil will befall you on that day. Your thirtieth birthday will come upon a Sunday.'"

"Well!" I queried, as the man paused.

"My thirtieth birthday as a fact did fall upon a Sunday," he said, with a bitter smile. "Curious that the old woman could have seen so far ahead in the almanack, was it not?"

"And nothing else happened, I presume?"

"Pardon me. My bad fortune was frequently talked about in the family—it was never wholly forgotten. After I married I told my wife of the prophecy. This morning when I left home she begged, entreated me to remain indoors. She had a presentiment that something ominous was about to happen, but I laughed at her fears."

"And your birthday—your thirtieth birthday, that has fallen——"

"My thirtieth birthday is to-day—Sunday—and to-day I am a prisoner," with which words he fell into a fit of despondency.

His wife came to see him—a very charming creature. She scolded him and kissed him in a breath. She told him again and again of her fears in his behalf, and she presented such a picture of distress that I couldn't help reflecting whether, unintentionally, I had contributed to her sorrow by delaying her husband's arrest to this fatal thirtieth anniversary of his birthday.

It was certainly very singular that I had obtained the clue, in the first instance, in such a casual way, and it was more than strange that, moved by some instinct—totally inexplicable—I delayed making the arrest until this very day. I might have taken the decisive step two or three months earlier, only I never had quite satisfied myself on the score of his identity until this fatal Sunday.

The accused was in due course charged, committed,

extradited, tried, and convicted of the offence of which he was accused, but all parties seemed more dismayed by the coincidence which I had set forth than by any other circumstances.

Yet not one of us then knew that they were perfectly right. The term of imprisonment which the convict duly served was the lightest part of his punishment. The curse fell upon him and his, root and branch. My pen falters as I approach the end. I dare not faithfully record the full measure of woe which descended upon that household and those who entered it.

When the convict emerged from gaol, perhaps with some hopes of a brighter life, having expiated the past, and looking forward to a return of the happy wedded life which he had previously enjoyed, he found that the woman he had worshipped had deserted him, and had transferred her affections, as he suspected, to another man.

The once happy home was broken up. Disaster followed upon disaster. It did not fall merely upon the man; it engulfed the woman, and her supposed betrayer. The retribution was complete. I dare not paint the picture. It is too awful It is the story of three ruined lives; and the grave has closed upon their misery

Of course, it may be said that the hand of fate had nothing to do with the Tascheritz disasters, and the prophecy on the part of the wise woman was a pure coincidence. That may have been so. Coincidence, as I have said, often crops up in crime. Here, for example, is another singular instance.

In connection with a certain notorious swindling case I had two men under observation, and requiring the assistance of an officer I scribbled a hurried note, and despatched it by a cabman to Scotland Yard, the men whom I was watching then being in a gambling club.

Now, as it happened, the officer who shortly arrived upon the scene to aid me in the arrest of these two men was Inspector Andrew Lansdowne—a strange coincidence, as will presently be seen.

Well, we captured the swindlers, and then began to search the house where one of the prisoners lived, and whilst engaged in that work my colleague took up a receipt for some cigars, the wife of one of the accused being present in the room.

This receipt was signed, "Fred Appleton."

"Fred Appleton!" exclaimed Lansdowne, and then turning to the woman, he asked, "Has he anything to do with the cigar merchant at Holloway?"

"Yes," replied the woman, "I believe he has."

"Does your husband know him?' was the next question.

She believed that he did; but, growing suddenly cautious, she refused to disclose what further information upon the subject she had.

Lansdowne, taking the first opportunity, told me that he was searching for this same "Fred Appleton," in connection with some very heavy robberies at the docks. I determined, therefore, to make use of the information given to us by the woman, if that proved at all possible.

One day, when my prisoner—the husband of the woman —was under remand at Bow Street, my opportunity came.

My man was very anxious that some money and jewellery, found in his possession at the time of his arrest, should be given to his wife. Now, there was no objection to this being done, but I raised obstacles, and as the prisoner grew very anxious, I said—

"Well, one good turn deserves another If I return this money and jewellery, tell me where to find Appleton."

He demurred for a very long time At last he said—

"You can hear of him at ——'s," mentioning a certain public-house, and he would say no more.

I visited the public-house in question whenever my business took me in that direction, and I found that Appleton was known by name to the potman and barmaids One day I was in the bar, talking with a man who had a good knowledge of all the shady characters in the neighbourhood, and of the frequenters of this tavern.

On my left I had observed three men in earnest conversation, and perceived that they were taking considerable notice of me. One of the trio I knew perfectly well, and he was drawing the attention of his companions to me in a particularly marked manner.

Suddenly all three men left the house.

At a favourable moment I then said casually to my acquaintance, "What has become of Appleton? does he come here now?"

"Why," he exclaimed, "he was here a moment ago" —pointing to the spot where the three men had been standing.

I passed the matter off, for my friend clearly saw that I was "pumping" him, but as soon as it was possible I left the house Of course the birds had flown; and although I returned to the rendezvous several times afterwards I never saw them there again.

About a week later, while journeying towards the City

on other business, I saw coming towards me two of the
men who had been in the public-house at the time I was
there. One of them corresponded with the description
of Appleton.

Instinctively I felt that they recognized me, and I
endeavoured to look as unconcerned as possible, fearing
that they would run away.

When the men were level with me, I suddenly turned
and said to the one I wanted—

"Your name is Appleton, I believe?"

"Yes, Mr. Littlechild" he replied, "I see you know me;"
and he took his arrest with the most perfect composure

CHAPTER XXII.

MORE COINCIDENCES IN CRIME—THE STORY OF A SUDDEN
TEMPTATION

"MR. LITTLECHILD," said my superior officer one
day to me at Scotland Yard, "just look over
these papers. I think I shall have to ask you to take the
case in hand. Inspector X—— had the inquiry before he
fell ill, and he has not made much of it so far."

Inspector X—— had, in fact, left the service in consequence of ill-health, so that I did not feel like treading
upon his toes in devoting my energies to the matter, and
in any case, of course, my duty was to obey my chief.

The reports passed over to me I discovered upon perusal
were of a very general character. They had been, before
they were placed in my hands, temporarily in those of
another officer, after X—— became incapacitated, but this
second man had been suddenly called away to undertake a
long journey abroad, and he had, previous to his departure,
not done very much.

I studied the records attentively, and then, according to
my rule, went over the ground to make myself fully acquainted with the details, in order, if possible, to carry the
matter to a successful conclusion.

The case related to a man in an influential position in the City of London, practising as an accountant, and having as well a yearly salary for a certain large firm whose books he audited. He appeared also to have had the control of a very large sum of money placed in trust, and the simple story was that, overcome by a sudden temptation, he had appropriated this money and made a bolt of it

This case was parallel with others which have come under my notice. Here was a man who had attained to years of discretion long before, and of irreproachable character, who, probably, repeatedly in his experience had been entrusted with money belonging to others, but who, nevertheless, on finding himself in control of a large sum, was unable to resist the craving to take it. The amount, although large, was not equal to his salary for five years capitalized.

Whenever I have met with such examples of men who are deficient in moral fibre when their slumbering cupidity is put to test, I have felt sorry for them. Their falling into crime I have never been able properly to account for, and it has invariably given me a keen sense of pain in carrying out the ultimate arrest.

However, I was a long way off this termination when I took the case up; for I did not know the whereabouts of Mr. Folly, the absconding accountant, at all.

I became aware, however, that, as a great many other men in similar cases had done before him, Mr. Folly had repented of the fraud he had committed; and had actually, through a friend, endeavoured to induce his former employers to withdraw from the prosecution, engaging that the money he had embezzled should be restored.

the firm very properly ignored such a compromise altogether.

The intermediary himself was a financial agent—Mr. Cute—and a close friend of the missing trustee, so obviously I could not approach him upon the subject; and I could make no use whatever of this clue to the whereabouts of the absconder.

When a deadlock thus confronted me, one day a clerk came to Scotland Yard and brought information about the case of another man who had taken to his heels with a view to evade the law.

"Mr. Littlechild," once again the superintendent said to me, "here is another absconding case. Just go up to Bow Street to procure a warrant on a sworn information, and execute it, if you can, for nothing is known of the man's whereabouts."

"What is the name?" was one of my first questions.

"Cute," replied the clerk, "too jolly 'cute by half. He has bolted with thousands."

"Cute!" I echoed, much astonished, and then suddenly checked myself, for this was none other than the name of the intermediary who had been vainly endeavouring to procure an abandonment of the proceedings in the case against his friend the absconding trustee. It was a strange coincidence. Two men had fallen victims to the same temptation, and I was charged with the arrest of both.

It was not only a strange coincidence, but one which led to unexpected results. Criminals often find coincidence goes against them; indeed, it is simply another name for retributive justice.

Mr. Cute had a partner—a man of the highest integrity;

but a detective has to feel his way, and it was a little while after having been brought into close contact with him before I said to him—

"I believe, sir, it is in your power to render me some assistance in this case."

"I should be pleased to do what is in my power What do you wish to know?" he replied frankly.

"Has your partner left behind him in your office any documents which do not come within the scope of the business of the firm?"

"Oh yes, certainly He had a table of his own"

"May I ask you whether you have seen any papers referring to a Mr. Folly?"

"No. But there are some letters which are hieroglyphics to me—I don't understand them at all."

"Will you permit me to see them?"

Mr. Cute's partner readily consented, and in due course I was shown these papers. They represented a correspondence between Folly and Cute, in which the former asked his friend to effect the compromise by engaging to return the stolen money. The whole matter was mysteriously written, so that there was no wonder that Cute's partner could not comprehend it. To me, with my knowledge of the case, it was as clear as daylight.

I confided to the partner of the absent Cute the story as far as I knew it, and asked him if he would help me, and he willingly promised to assist the ends of justice.

But when he came to hunt for Folly's address we could find no trace of it. Cute must have destroyed every paper which contained it.

"There is no address," cried the partner. "How can I help you?"

"A course has occurred to me," I replied, "which I should wish to adopt."

I was very anxious to secure Folly's arrest, because there was a good reward, which is always a stimulus to energy. Perhaps I ought here to explain that I regarded Folly as my man, and not Cute. Cute has never been seen from that day to this, but for reasons which I need not enter upon here the case against him was dropped and the hunt in reality was for Folly alone.

Proceeding to explain my scheme to Cute's partner, I said—

"This was Mr. Cute's room?"

"Yes," he replied, "my partner sat at that table"

"Will you obtain for me a specimen of his handwriting and of his signature?"

There was no difficulty on his part in complying with my request.

"Now," said I, as I took the papers handed to me, "I want one of Mr. Cute's pens—one that he has recently used."

The partner looked at me in some surprise, but gave me what I required without a word. He was evidently becoming interested.

"I will tell you what I am about to do," I explained. "There is one person in London who knows the address of the fugitive Folly." (I had gathered this from the reports sent in connection with Folly) "He is a most confidential man, and I believe he is the only person, with the exception of your partner, who has this information in his possession. I am going to obtain Folly's address from that individual."

"But how are you to get it?" he asked.

" Wait," I said.

I then sat down at Cute's desk, took his pen, and, with his writing and signature before me, wrote, in imitation of Cute's hand, the following letter :—

" With regard to the matter of your friend" (meaning Folly), "I have now seen the securities, and they have at last agreed to the compromise, and everything can be satisfactorily settled. I am writing to F. to-night, but thought that you would like to know this as early as possible."

I then added my copy of the signature of the absconding Mr. Cute, and addressed the envelope to the man of whom I had spoken as being the only person in London who knew Folly's address.

I may say that this incident happened so soon after the second absconding—that of Cute himself—that I felt certain, as the matter had not got into the papers, the man to whom I was now writing would not be aware of the deception I was practising upon him, or have heard of Cute's disappearance

I reopened the letter and added the following P.S. .—

" I have had to reopen this, for on writing my letter to F. I find that I have stupidly, in destroying some papers the other day, torn up his address. Let me have it by return of post, as I wish to relieve his mind as early as possible."

I added Cute's initials.

Perhaps it may astonish some people that I should have attempted to imitate a man's handwriting at such short notice, but I may say that I had practised it frequently. It is necessary that you should use the man's own pen, which perserves in a singular manner the characteristics of his writing. You could not do it with your own pen, but with the pen which has been actually employed by the person whose handwriting you wish to imitate it is wonderful what results may be obtained.

When Cute's partner saw my imitations and read the letter, he exclaimed—

"By Jove, that is immense! That will bring it!"

"No," said I, "it won't. That is only the stepping-stone. I want to ask one other favour. Will you let me represent your partner to-morrow? That letter will not bring the address, but it will bring the man here, and it is within my knowledge that he does not know Mr. Cute except by name."

"I think you are right," said the gentleman.

Accordingly it was arranged that on the following day I should act the part of financial agent, and the clerks were warned that if Mr. So-and-So called he was to be shown into the room, where I was to sit, black-coated and otherwise made up to represent the part, busied with Cute's papers.

The morning came. I took my place at the table and waited for the man to whom I had written in Cute's name.

Of course he would not address a letter through the post, but he duly called, and was ushered in to hold a conversation with, as he believed, his correspondent Cute.

My visitor was delighted to hear of the result of the negotiations in Folly's case, undertaken by his friend Cute.

I apologized for troubling him for Folly's address, and talked to him generally about his case, displaying an intimate knowledge of its points, and talking very glibly, on

Q

the strength of the information I had been able to acquire. My behaviour evidently allayed his suspicions, and he at length, believing that I was Cute himself, communicated to me the much-wanted address.

He left the office, and so did I. The first cab took me to Scotland Yard, and the next train to Wales conveyed me to a pleasant little watering-place

There I ascertained that under another name a gentleman had been living genteelly and quietly at the address which had been given to me. It appeared that my man had been "on the wing" for some time, but had at last settled down in Wales.

I spent the day with a person who was able to point him out to me, but it was a day of suspense. I relied, however, upon a circumstance which has often served usefully in such a case of patient watching

At dusk most people light the gas before the blinds are pulled down, disclosing to the man who is keeping a house under observation a full view of the occupants of the rooms. Waiting thus for the gloaming in a convenient spot, we watched for the gas to be lighted. In a word, my man was identified and the arrest was made.

"How did he take it?" I have been asked.

Very quietly. It was a relief to him, and his expression was, "I'm thankful I am arrested at last!" His was just one other case of that class of men who, having yielded to sudden temptation and fled with their spoil, are overtaken by remorse and are yet fearful of being caught. In every bush they see a detective, and finally the poor hunted wretch exclaims, "Would to Heaven that death or a detective would come!"

CHAPTER XXIII., AND LAST.

A GHOSTLY ADVENTURE.

THERE was great consternation at Pendennick Castle, in Cornwall, the seat of Lord Pendennick—as for the purposes of this narrative I shall call him.

All the family jewels had been stolen, and apart from the value of the heirlooms, which are always priceless to their possessors, and that of the countess's coronet, the loss was estimated at £20,000.

In post haste I was hurried down to Pendennick, for the local police were at fault, and at the time of which I write—not so very long ago either—it was not unusual for the assistance of Scotland Yard to be obtained in such an emergency.

I did not arrive upon the scene until forty-eight hours after the robbery had been perpetrated—for it was not a burglary, in the technical sense, as burglaries only take place between sundown and sunrise. Nor was it, as far as I could tell, a case of housebreaking. In fact, the whole matter was involved in mystery of the most aggravating kind.

Lord Pendennick received me very kindly, and immediately ordered that my requests should be observed

"May I see," said I, "everything in the exact position in which it was when the robbery was first discovered?"

Accordingly, I was conducted to his lordship's dressing-room and to her ladyship's bedroom. From these two rooms the jewels had, I was told, mysteriously disappeared. They had been abstracted from cabinets, and these I carefully examined; but I detected no sign of a broken or picked lock, a forced-open drawer, or the marks of any instrument such as "cracksmen" use.

"Were these cabinets locked at the time?" I naturally asked.

"They should have been," was the answer, "and we believe they were."

"Do you keep the keys, my lord?"

"Well, I don't carry them about with me," the earl replied. "Her ladyship's maid sometimes requires them, of course."

I made a mental note of that point. Next I scrutinized the doors of both bedrooms very minutely. There was no mark of their having been wedged, or otherwise secured from within.

"These doors," I asked, "were found locked?"

"Not at all," replied the earl; "they were open—wide open."

We were then standing in the dressing-room, which was lighted by a window overlooking some leads, the roof of the billiard-room or study on ground floor. This frontage of the house was castellated. The window was open, and I stepped lightly upon the leads. Around one of the buttresses of the embattlement was a rope, in a slip-knot, and the end dangled to the ground below.

I pulled it up and tested its strength. It was sound and strong—quite strong enough to bear the weight of a man.

"That is how he got away," interjected the local police-officer who had accompanied me on my first inspection of the scene.

"Who—the burglar?"

"Yes,' he answered officiously.

"When was it—at what time of the day was this robbery first discovered?" was my next question.

"On Sunday, during church time," the earl replied.

"Would there have been people moving about in the park at that hour?" I queried.

"Very possibly.'

"And the castle, I see, occupies an eminence. There are no trees at this corner, and if the burglar wished to make his escape as public as possible, he would have descended by this rope."

"Ah! then you think he might have been seen?"

"He stood that risk, certainly," I said.

"But if he didn't go down by the rope, what did he want it for?" put in the sagacious member of the county constabulary.

"It is not unlikely he provided the rope as a means of escape, supposing that he found it dangerous to make his exit by the ordinary way; or he may have lowered the jewels to the ground to a confederate waiting below," I suggested.

"But why should he not have used the rope himself?" persisted the policeman.

"There was no necessity for him to have done so," I said. Then, turning to his lordship, I asked, "Am I right in supposing, my lord, that on Sunday morning the front door by which I entered, and which leads to the great staircase at the end of the hall, was open?"

"Quite so," the earl replied.

"Then that was the way by which the thief came in."

"You have a reason for coming to that conclusion?" he asked.

"My reason, my lord, is that it is the more probable explanation. I notice that the window of this dressing-room has a hasp inside. The window is usually opened from the top, and not from below—for the condition of the paint indicates it. This window was opened from below on Sunday for the first time since it was repainted. Now observe, there are no tool marks upon the sash to indicate that it has been forced from outside. Again, there is the rope."

"Well, what does the rope show?" queried his lordship, keenly interested.

"The slip-knot—which I was careful not to disturb in testing the rope—is of a kind which indicates plainly enough that it was placed deliberately around the buttress by some one standing on the leads above. It was not thrown as a lasso, from below over the stonework, and I am certain no man has descended by it, for if it had borne the weight of a man the rope would have been pulled taut, and perhaps been frayed by the sharp edge of this masonry, whereas it is perfectly clean and quite loose—you see."

We went downstairs. The hall door was still open, and I went outside and walked upon the lawn. I saw the hanging rope plainly: it crossed a window.

"Is that the window of the billiard-room?" I asked.

"No, that is my study adjoining it. I was sitting there when the robbery was discovered, reading," said the earl; "I was not at church."

"Then you must of necessity have been disturbed by some one clambering down the rope from above."

"I should have heard him, I suppose'

Convinced that the thief could not have made use of the rope for that purpose, I turned my attention next to an examination of the other means of escape

It seemed quite possible that a practised hand could have entered the hall unperceived, and relying upon his knowledge that the servants would have left the rooms to air, and were busy downstairs whilst the family were at church, had simply walked up the staircase and appropriated the jewels But this theory depended first upon his ability to get into the park unaccosted—a point which I reserved for fuller inquiry—and next upon the exact information which he possessed as to the rooms in which the jewels were kept and the cabinets in which they were concealed.

Had the thief a confederate?

Now, I know whenever a jewel robbery occurs at a country house, there is a common notion that the thieves must have been assisted by one or more of the servants. But I desire to place on record my belief that this is entirely erroneous. A thief is not likely to lay himself open to betrayal at the hands of a domestic when it is possible to obtain all the information he requires much more readily. He has, in most cases, merely to act upon his common sense in selecting a time when the family is at dinner—a quiet meal, not a dress one, for the more homely the occasion the less probable is it that the upstairs rooms will be tenanted or that the jewels will be in use The thief knows, too, that valuables are not kept as a rule downstairs

In my experience I have found that in high-class houses the men-servants are a very respectable body. It is true a butler or footman may be guilty sometimes of larceny, but he rarely associates himself with the professional thief or burglar. Women servants, too, have little chance of making the acquaintance of such a man, with a view to introducing him into the houses of their masters.

But at Pendennick Castle the circumstances were out of the ordinary run of things. Sunday morning was a strange time to select, and it was plain that the cabinets had been opened by some one who needed neither false keys nor jemmy

I do not know for what reason the local police acted in this manner—but when I began to inquire about each of the servants, and to take from them a statement in writing as to their whereabouts on the morning of the robbery, I found that two of the principal witnesses were already in custody.

They were a valet and a lady's-maid, and the case against them was one of ordinary suspicion. All that could be alleged against them was that they were the last to have entered the dressing-room and bedroom from which the jewels had been taken

For some hours I was engaged in taking in statements in detail, the steward's room having been placed at my disposal. When night time came I was very tired.

The earl had himself ordered a room to be prepared for me in the castle, although I had left my luggage at the village hotel, which was at some distance. It was more convenient that I should remain in the castle, where much remained to be done, and my portmanteau was sent for.

After supper a man-servant conducted me to my bed-chamber. I then began to realize the immense size of Pendennick Castle. We traversed corridor after corridor, barely illuminated by the flickering light of the taper which my guide held. I lost all count of direction.

Finally the man-servant opened a door, and we passed into a long gallery, or armoury, which appeared to occupy the front of a whole wing of the castle. It was a cold, clear winter's night, and there was a sharp, frosty moon Its beams, parting through the tracery of the windows, cast intricate shadows upon the polished floor Here and there they fell upon the glint of steel and upon shadowy figures which occupied deep recesses between the casements.

The opposite wall was pierced by several doorways, facing the great windows. Through them I beheld in the silvery light a beautiful view of the park, its great oaks and giant elms casting dark shadows upon the sward. It was a ghostly, eerie place—not a place in which to be left alone at the "witching hour of night," at a time of the year when departed spirits are supposed to have the free run of this earth.

I was ushered into my room. It was in the corner tower. I stumbled down two steps and found myself in a comfortable bedroom, very cosy with its curtains and hangings, antique furniture, and sweet-smelling, cheerful wood-fire glowing in the huge grate.

The servant handed me a candle, bade me "good-night," saying, "I think you will be comfortable here," and took his leave. I heard his footfall echo along the deserted gallery. A door closed with a bang, awakening a succession of weird whisperings, and then all was silence.

I was left alone in a wing of the castle in which there was no other living soul.

I sat by the warm fire for a while and then went to bed. But I could not sleep. My mind was too full of the case which had so far perplexed me.

"What is the meaning of that rope?" I thought, without being able to dismiss the interrogation from my mind or find a satisfactory answer to it—except the supposition that it had been placed there as a "blind," merely to deceive people into the belief that a burglary had been committed

Was it done by the servants, or by whom?

As sleep would not come, I thought I would take a turn in the ghostly gallery—to explore it. So I left my bed, put on some clothing, and went into the gallery. The moonlight was still fitfully throwing fairy frescoes upon the floor I walked to the window and looked out upon a noble expanse of park. There were dark clouds scudding across the brilliant orb in the dark-blue heavens, and alternately the swards were in deep shadow and brightest light. It was a pretty picture.

Suddenly, as I gazed, the moon just then disappearing into a bank of cloud, I saw—or fancied I saw—a figure clothed in white, flit from a great oak which spread its branches in a huge circle. The figure—it was that of a woman—hurried to an elm, which was nearer to the castle wall, and then I saw it no more

There was a peculiar soft tread like that of a cat heard at that instant in the gallery. I sank back into one of the recesses between the windows, and recoiled as I felt the cold touch of steel.

I had pushed against one of the mail-clad effigies which adorned the place.

Speedily recovering myself, I waited—waited for the ghostly pit-a-pat. In the light of the moon which then burst into the gallery, was it mere imagination that I saw a black form slowly making its way towards my room?

There was a singular preoccupied look upon the face of this man—for man it was—as he passed me, never seeing me, and there was a strange movement of his hands. He seemed to be wringing them dry, or cleansing them of dust.

Cautiously he went to my door, appeared to listen, and then, turning, retraced his way precisely as he had come, always flicking the dust from his fingers and rubbing off the invisible mire.

I saw the man's face plainly I had not seen it before in the castle among all the servants I had closely interrogated

Now, I am not one to be easily alarmed by spectral visions or imaginings due to an overwrought brain, and when I crept back to my bed it was with some feeling that what I had seen bore upon my case, but how I could not tell

Did it portend that I should have to satisfy myself that the servants were innocent?

As I turned the matter over in my mind—for I was wide awake still—I recalled a case in which I had been previously engaged when a certain noble lord required my assistance.

Lord S—— had been informed of a conspiracy to steal

his plate   I learned that a shoemaker, of rather doubtful antecedents, had the run of the butler's pantry, and to him a sweep had suggested that the aid of a professional thief should be obtained, with a view to carrying off the silver.

The shoemaker got frightened, and told his lordship about the plot. At my request the shoemaker continued to confer with the sweep, and, at the latter's request, consented to go with him to find an expert thief to do the job

Unknown to either, I "shadowed" them both, following them to town, sometimes to Marylebone, and at other times to Mint Street in the Borough.   I satisfied myself that the shoemaker had told the truth, and heard him on one occasion say to his confederate that he could not find the thieves because they were out of town on some big job

On one occasion the sweep had picked up with a burglar, and as this gentleman had been taken down to an inn near to Lord S——'s property, we thought it well not to wait longer ; but having obtained a warrant we arrested the sweep in i working clothes, and the soot ruined a nice new suit which my assistant happened to be wearing when he captured his man at close quarters.

"Now," I reflected, as I recalled this incident, "if the plate had really been stolen by the burglar, the servants in the household, and not the sweep or shoemaker, would have been wrongfully suspected as confederates. It may be so again here."

I was glad when daylight came.   That morning, and for many days, I was engaged in my investigation. Having exhausted my inquiries in the household, without finding any explanation for the extraordinary incidents of the first

night of my visit in the castle, I made inquiries at the
nearest railway station, at the farmhouses, in the village,
and at every spot where men congregated, to discover if
any stranger had been seen in the vicinity of the castle,
but every one declared that no one had been noticed

Then as regards access to the park, it was not forbidden
to the public, but the right-of-way was limited to a footpath
which crossed the grounds of the castle at some distance
from the building itself It was probable that the thief
might have used this footpath.

It was next my duty to ransack the castle from cellar to
roof—an almost interminable task, involving the exploration
of musty garrets and mildewed cellars; of poking and
prying into old linen-presses, dusty cupboards, and iron-
chests; of sounding oaken wainscoting for secret panels;
of hunting here, there, and everywhere, but without result,
for the missing jewels were still undiscovered

Many a night I listened in the deserted armoury, hoping
for a repetition of the vision of the white-robed damsel who
flitted from the oak to the elm, and of the strange man
who kept flicking the dust off his hands in the great
gallery. But I never saw either the woman or the man
again.

I have told my story. It is that of a failure and not one
of a success. Detectives are not always able to discover
mysteries. Time alone can solve some.

It has solved this one—to an extent.

Many months after I had returned to Scotland Yard
from Cornwall, somewhat disheartened with the unsatisfactory result of my labours, there was a discovery made
at Pendennick Castle. In a heap of rubbish, which we

had partially sifted, one day a labourer unearthed a box. That box contained the missing family jewels.

But who had placed them there in that place of hiding? Whether it was done by a somnambulist, the man I had seen rubbing invisible mire from his hands, or by a servant who had been discharged before she was able to take the property away with her, I cannot tell   And what about my vision?

Well; I may have been a victim of my own imagination, and that is why I have not cared hitherto to dwell upon the strangest and most unaccountable part of this story

THE END.

EXTRACTS FROM

The Leadenhall Press
Book List.

THE LEADENHALL PRESS, Ltd:

50, LEADENHALL STREET, LONDON, E C.

IMPRINTED AT THE LEADENHALL PRESS, LTD: LONDON

The Best **Book of Alphabets** Published.

A NEW SHILLING

Book of

Alphabets

Plain & Ornamental,
Ancient and Modern,

For the Use of Draughtsmen,

Clergymen,

Decorators,

Designers,

ARCHITECTS,

Teachers, &c.

With a curiously inter-
esting and complete
Alphabet (capitals and
small letters) in fac-
simile from an original
MS. written by CHARLES I.,
together with his writing-
master's "copy."

LONDON: The Leadenhall Press, Ltd: 50, Leadenhall Street, E.C.

(3)

By Command Dedicated to ☐☐☐ *Her Majesty the Queen*

THE FOLLIES AND FASHIONS OF OUR GRAND-
FATHERS (1807) Embellished with Thirty-seven whole-page Plates of Ladies' and Gentlemen's Dress (hand coloured and heightened with gold and silver), Sporting and Coaching Scenes, &c., &c. By ANDREW W TUER LONDON The Leadenhall Press, Ltd 50, Leadenhall-street, E C

> Large Paper copies, crown 4to, with *earliest impressions* of the plates, 250 only, signed and numbered, at Three Guineas (Nearly out of print)
> Demy 8vo copies at Twenty five Shillings (Out of print)

EXTRA ILLUSTRATED
COLLECTORS' EDITION IN FOUR VOLUMES
FIFTY COPIES ONLY, SIGNED AND NUMBERED

By Command Dedicated to ☐☐☐ *Her Majesty the Queen*

BARTOLOZZI AND HIS WORKS Biographical, Anecdotal
and Descriptive By ANDREW W TUER Illustrated [The two volume edition is out of print] This special edition—in four stout handsome vellum bound quarto volumes, on extra thick paper—is interleaved with guards or slips for the insertion of extra prints, and in addition to all the original illustrations contains SIXTEEN EXTRA PRINTS in fine bright condition of the following attractive subjects of the Bartolozzi school Spring, Summer, Autumn, Winter, a set of four, Adoration, Mrs Cosway, Hon Mrs Damer, Master Thornhill, Light as Love, Cherubs, Loves, a pair, Cupid Sharpening his Arrows, Paris and Œnone, Ceres and Pomona, a pair. LONDON The Leadenhall Press, Ltd 50, Leadenhall-street, E C　　　　　　[Six Guineas
(Octavo edition in one volume, Twelve-and-Sixpence)

NEW EDITION OF
MRS GREET'S STORY OF THE GOLDEN OWL With
twenty-four whole page Illustrations by AMBROSE DUDLEY LON-DON The Leadenhall Press, Ltd 50, Leadenhall street, E C
　　　　　　　　　　　　　　　　　[Three-and-Sixpence

MRS. DORA GREET'S STORY OF THE GOLDEN OWL.
With twenty-four whole page illustrations by AMBROSE DUDLEY LONDON The Leadenhall Press, Ltd 50, Leadenhall Street, E C
　　　　　　　　　　　　　　　　　[Six Shillings
Printed on brown paper throughout A most remarkable book both in matter and manner

---

ENGLISH COUNTY SONGS (Words and Music.) Col-
lected and Edited by LUCY E BROADWOOD and J A FULLER MAIT LAND, M A , F S A LONDON The Leadenhall Press, Ltd 50, Leadenhall street, E C.
　　　　　　　　　　　　　　　　　[Six Shillings

IN JEST AND EARNEST · A BOOK OF GOSSIP. By
JOSEPH HATTON, author of "The Reminiscences of J L. Toole," "Henry Irving's Impressions of America," "Clytie," "By Order of the Czar," "The Princess Mazaroff," &c With a Prefatory Address to his friend, J L Toole LONDON The Leadenhall Press, Ltd 50, Leadenhall street, E C　　　　　　　　[Two-and-Sixpence

(5)

(6)

(7)

The ten whole page Illustrations, from the ORIGINAL copper-plates (since destroyed), are delicately hand coloured in Rowlandson's style, and include the diligence or mail coach changing horses on a road paced with rough cobble stones, fashionable persons, male and female, in quaint costumes of the period, cabriolet or vehicle apparently the precursor of the modern hansom cab, a conjuror and his assistant, female quack medicine vendor, &c, &c

250 Copies only, each one numbered and signed.

Copper plates destroyed

MANNERS AND CUSTOMS OF THE FRENCH (fac-simile of the scarce 1875 edition), with ten whole page amusing and prettily tinted Illustrations LONDON The Leadenhall Press, Ltd 50, Leadenhall-street, E C   [Sixteen Shillings

---

COUNSEL TO LADIES AND EASY-GOING MEN ON THEIR BUSINESS INVESTMENTS, and cautions against the lures of Wily Financiers and Unprincipled promoters LONDON The Leadenhall Press, Ltd 50, Leadenhall Street, London, E C
[Three-and Sixpence

" The price of the book is 3s 6d, and is in itself an excellent investment "—*Sala's Journal*

THE CHILD SET IN THE MIDST By MODERN POETS ("*And He took a little child and set him in the midst of them*') Edited by WILFRID MEYNELL With a facsimile of the MS of "The Toys," by COVENTRY PATMORE LONDON The Leadenhall Press, Ltd 50, Leadenhall street, E C   [Six Shillings

---

FROM THE BULL'S POINT OF VIEW THE TRUE STORY OF A BULL FIGHT. By R. ST JOHN CORBET.
LONDON The Leadenhall Press, Ltd 50, Leadenhall street, E C
[Sixpence.

SPLAY-FEET SPLASHINGS IN DIVERS PLACES By GOOSESTEP. LONDON The Leadenhall Press, Ltd 50, Leadenhall street, E C   [Three and Sixpence.

BRIC-À-BRAC BALLADS By GOOSESTEP, author of "Splay Feet Splashings in Divers Places" LONDON The Leadenhall Press, Ltd 50, Leadenhall street, E C   [One Shilling.

JOE MILLER IN MOTLEY, BEING THE CREAM OF JOE'S JESTS Compiled by W CAREW HAZLITT LONDON The Leadenhall Press, Ltd 50, Leadenhall street, E C   [Two Shillings.

ENGLISH CAROLS OF THE FIFTEENTH CENTURY from a MS Roll in the Library of Trinity College, Cambridge Edited by J A FULLER MAITLAND, M A, F S A, with added Vocal Parts by W S ROCKSTRO Frontispiece facsimile in colours of the "Agincourt Song," No VII LONDON The Leadenhall Press, Ltd 50, Leadenhall street, E C   [Ten Shillings.

SECOND EDITION.

TRICKS AND TRICKSTERS. Tales founded on fact from a Lawyer's Note-Book. By JOSEPH FORSTER, author of "Some French and Spanish Men of Genius," "Four great Teachers Carlyle, Ruskin, Emerson, and Browning," "Duty Wins," &c LONDON The Leadenhall Press, Ltd 50, Leadenhall street, E C   [One Shilling

(8)

"I have got a new-born sister,
I was nigh the first that kiss'd her"

(CHARLES and MARY LAMB)

POETRY FOR CHILDREN, entirely original, by the Author of "Mrs Leicester's School" In two volumes A facsimile, including both frontispieces specially engraved on copper, of the extremely scarce original 1809 edition In a pretty contemporary binding by Zaehnsdorf The copies are limited to 100, each numbered and signed. LONDON The Leadenhall Press, Ltd 50, Leadenhall street, E C
[£1 10s the two volumes, nett

THE DOLLS' GARDEN PARTY By JAMES M LOWRY Author of "The Keys at Home," &c, &c Illustrated by J B CLARK LONDON The Leadenhall Press, Ltd 50, Leadenhall Street, L C
[Half a Crown

A STORY OF STOPS By Mrs DAVIDSON, of Tulloch, author of "Kitten's Goblins" Prettily Illustrated by the authoress. LONDON The Leadenhall Press, Ltd 50, Leadenhall street, F C
[Five Shillings

KITTEN'S GOBLINS By Mrs DAVIDSON, of Tulloch With a dozen whole page illustrations by the authoress LONDON The Leadenhall Press, Ltd 50, Leadenhall street, E C.
[Five Shillings.

THROUGH ENGLAND ON A SIDE-SADDLE IN THE TIME OF WILLIAM & MARY, being the diary of CELIA FIENNES With an explanatory Introduction by The Hon Mrs GRIFFITHS LONDON The Leadenhall Press, Ltd 50, Leadenhall street, E C
[Twelve and-Sixpence

THE ORACLES OF NOSTRADAMUS. By CHAS A WARD LONDON The Leadenhall Press, Ltd 50, Leadenhall-street, E.C.
[Six Shillings
Contains a round hundred, or more, out of the thousand quatrains of the French prophet, that, since his death, have all received startling fulfilment in history.

"THOSE FOREIGN DEVILS!" A CELESTIAL ON ENGLAND AND ENGLISHMEN, Edited by W H. WILKINSON, H M Consular Service, China. LONDON The Leadenhall Press, Ltd 50, Leadenhall street, E C
[Two and-Sixpence

THE STAGE IN THE DRAWING-ROOM SHORT ONE-ACT SKETCHES FOR TWO AND THREE PLAYERS BY MILLIE SELOUS. LONDON The Leadenhall Press, Ltd 50, Leadenhall street, E C
[Half a-Crown.

JOHN BULL JUNIOR: or FRENCH AS SHE IS TRADUCED Enlarged from 'Drat the Boys!" By MAX O'RELL, author of "John Bull and his Island," &c LONDON The Leadenhall Press, Ltd 50, Leadenhall-street, E.C
[One Shilling.

JOHN BULL AND HIS ISLAND. (Cheap Edition) Translated from the French by the Author, MAX O'RELL LONDON The Leadenhall Press, Ltd 50, Leadenhall-street, E C [One Shilling
Upwards of two hundred thousand copies have been disposed of.

(9)

DRAT THE BOYS! or, R COLLFCTIONS OF AN FX-FRENCH
MASTER IN ENC AND By MAX O'RELL, author of "John Bull and
his Island," &c, &c LONDON The Leadenhall Press, Ltd 50,
Leadenhall street, EC [Two Shillings

LAYS OF A LAZY LAWYER By AL-SO
LONDON The Leadenhall Press, Ltd 50, Leadenl all street, E C.
[One Shilling

DRINKS OF THE WORLD WINES, SPIRITS, LIQUEURS,
BEFI, TEA, COFFEE, COCOA, MILK, SPARKLING AND MISCELLANE-
OUS DRINKS By JAMES MEW and JOHN ASHTON One Hundred
Illustrations LONDON The Leadenhall Press, Ltd 50, Leadenhall
street, L C [One Guinea

"THE GRASSHOPPER," being some account of the Banking House at 63, Lombard Street By JOHN BIDDULPH MAR. ,
M A, F S S Illustrated LONDON The Leadenhall Press, Ltd
50, Leadenhall street, E C [One Guinea

THE DAINTIEST OF DAINTY BOOKS
BYGONE BEAUTIES PAINTED BY HOPPNER ten
delicately engraved portraits of beautiful women of a bygone
period Introduction by ANDREW W TUER, F S A LONDON The
Leadenhall Press, Ltd 50, Leadenhall street. E C [Two Shillings

---

76th THOUSAND
OLD LONDON STREET CRIES AND THE CRIES OF
TO DAY, with heaps of Quaint Cuts, including hand coloured frontis
piece By ANDREW W TUER, F S A, author of "Bartolozzi and
his Works," &c LONDON The Leadenhall Press, Ltd 50, Leadenhall street, E C [One Shilling
"Very amusing. Charmingly pretty A wonderful shilling's-
worth "—*Globe.*

NEW AND ENLARGED EDITION
HANDBOOK OF LONDON BANKERS, with Some
Account of their Predecessors the Early Goldsmiths, together with
List of Bankers from 1070, &c, &c By F. G HILTON PRICE, F S A
LONDON The Leadenhall Press, Ltd 50, Leadenhall street, E C
[Fifteen Shillings

HOW TO FAIL IN LITERATURE A Lecture.
By ANDREW LANG Revised, corrected and augmented LONDON
The Leadenhall Press, Ltd 50, Leadenhall street, E C.
[One Shilling

JOHN OLDCASTLE'S GUIDE FOR LITERARY
BEGINNERS LONDON The Leadenhall Press, Ltd 50, Leadenhall-street, E C [One Shilling.
"Is the only practical and common sense book on the subject
we know of "

THE GRIEVANCES BETWEEN AUTHORS AND
PUBLISHERS, being the Report of the Conferences of the Incor-
porated Society of Authors held in Willis's Rooms in March, 1887,
with Additional Matter and Summary. LONDON · The Leadenhall
Press, Ltd 50, Leadenhall-street, E C [One Shilling

Dedicat by Permission to Admiral H R H The Duke of Edinburgh, K G.

REAL SAILOR-SONGS (Two-hundred Illustrations) Collected and edited by JOHN ASHTON, author of "A Century of Ballads," "Romances of Chivalry," &c, &c LONDON The Leadenhall Press, Ltd 50, Leadenhall street, E C.   [One Guinea

A magnificent volume profusely illustrated with the quaintest old woodcuts imaginable Many of these songs—originally sold in the streets—are reprinted in their pristine narrow form, being separately mounted on brown paper slips or guards The book is a monument of research and a triumph of the typographic art —*Daily Telegraph*

CHEAP EDITION

MODERN MEN By A MODERN MAID CONTENTS The Decay of Courtesy, Our Partners, Our Fellow Boarders, Husbands and Brothers, The Vanity of Men, Men and Money Matters, Objectionable Lovers, &c., &c LONDON The Leadenhall Press, Ltd 50, Leadenhall street, E C.   [One Shilling

A book in which modern men are amusingly abused

"CORNERED." By NORMAN PORRITT LONDON · The Leadenhall Press, Ltd 50, Leadenhall street, E C.

[Two-and Sixpence

AS THE WIND BLOWS By J PERCY KING LONDON The Leadenhall Press, Ltd 50, Leadenhall-street, E C

[Five Shillings

CURIOUS OLD COOKERY RECEIPTS, including Simples for Simple Ailments Printed from a Manuscript now dropping to pieces through much thumbing Frontispiece, an old inscribed pewter platter dated 1679 LONDON The Leadenhall Press, Ltd 50, Leadenhall street, E C.   [One Shilling

---

THE AUSTRALIAN AT HOME Notes and Anecdotes of Life at the Antipodes, including Useful Hints to those intending to Settle in Australia By EDWARD KINGLAKE LONDON The Leadenhall Press, Ltd 50, Leadenhall street, E C

[Two and Sixpence

DAME WIGGINS OF LEE Hand-coloured Illustrations LONDON · The Leadenhall Press, Ltd 50, Leadenhall street, E C.

[One Shilling

A Reprint of a picture book—illustrated from the original blocks, hand-coloured—used by our grandmothers when young. DAME WIGGINS OF LEE has met with the strong approval of Mr. Ruskin.

TALES OF THE "WILD AND WOOLLY WEST" By ADAIR WELCKER, of Berkeley, California LONDON The Leadenhall Press, Ltd. 50, Leadenhall street, E C   [One Shilling

(II)

PRINCE DORUS. By CHARLES LAMB A reproduction of the first edition of 1811, including all the beautiful coloured plates LONDON The Leadenhall Press, Ltd 50, Leadenhall street, E C

[Seven and Sixpence.

Five hundred copies only printed, each being separately numbered & signed.

A copy of this scarce and amusing book for children was recently sold by auction for £45

"This bright little volume will have a place in every collection of modern literary curiosities."—*Notes and Queries.*

CHEAP EDITION

PRINCE DORUS By CHARLES LAMB A reproduction of the scarce and pretty first edition of 1811, including all the coloured plates With Introduction by ANDREW W TUER, F S.A LONDON The Leadenhall Press, Ltd 50, Leadenhall street, E C [One Shilling

---

BEAUTY AND THE BEAST. By CHARLES LAMB. With an Introduction by ANDREW LANG Illustrated with eight beautiful steel plates engraved in facsimile from the original edition LONDON: The Leadenhall Press, Ltd 50, Leadenhall street, E C

[Three-and-Sixpence

A charming book of equal interest to children and their elders

One hundred signed copies only, containing a set of earliest open letter proofs of the eight illustrations in red, and a duplicate set in brown [Ten-and-Sixpence now raised to Two Guineas

---

GRAY'S ELEGY · with Sixteen beautiful Illustrations by NORMAN PRESCOTT DAVIES, facsimiled from his original drawings in the possession, and published by the gracious permission of H R H The PRINCESS OF WALES Bound in gold lettered vellum, with broad silken bands and strings LONDON The Leadenhall Press, Ltd 50 Leadenhall street, E.C. [One Guinea

"A work of very great beauty —*Leeds Mercury*

THE BANTAMS OF SHEFFIELD, a Novel. By GUY BALGUY, author of "The Maids of Dulverton" &c LONDON The Leadenhall Press, Ltd 50, Leadenhall-street, E C [Half a-Crown.

THE A. B. C. MARINERS' GUIDE, containing Complete Information relating to the Mercantile and Maritime Laws and Customs, including a useful set of Tables, &c, compiled by CAPTAIN R T STEVENS (Second Edition.) LONDON The Leadenhall Press, Ltd 50, Leadenhall street, E C [Seven-and Sixpence.

TABLE OF DISTANCES TO AND FROM THE Principal Commercial Seaports of the World shewing the distances in nautical miles both viâ the Capes and the Suez Canal, including a Table of Distances in the Sea of Marmora, the Black Sea and the Sea of Azof Compiled and arranged by CAPTAIN R T STEVENS

This Table shews at a glance the distance from anchorage to anchorage between the ports of London, Liverpool Newcastle, Cardiff and the principal commercial ports of the world, as also the distance of the latter ports from each other The distances given are the shortest possible in safe water

Price 30s., or mounted on linen 35s., mounted on linen, rollers and varnished 40s

LONDON The Leadenhall Press, Ltd 50, Leadenhall-street, E.C.

A TABLE OF DISTANCES IN NAUTICAL MILES between the principal ports of the United Kingdom, and ports in the North Sea, Kattegat, Baltic Sea and Gulfs of Finland and Bothnia. Compiled by CAPTAIN R T STEVENS. LONDON The Leadenhall Press, Ltd 50, Leadenhall street, E C   [Two Shillings

---

OXFORD TO PALESTINE. Be   Notes of a Tour made in the Autumn of 1889 By the Rev   PH LL THOMAS, M A, Briton Ferry   Author of "An Under uate's Trip to Italy and Attica" LONDON The Leadenh ll Press, Ltd 50, Leadenhall-street, E C.   [Two-and-Sixpence.

UP THE MOONSTAIR, a Story for Children. By ALBERT E HOOPER, with Twelve Illustrations by HARRY PARKES LONDON The Leadenhall Press, Ltd 50, Leadenhall-street, E C   [Three-and Sixpence

---

RUS IN URBE: or FLOWERS THAT THRIVE IN LONDON GARDENS AND SMOKY TOWNS By M E HARRIS   Illustrated LONDON. The Leadenhall Press, Ltd 50, Leadenhall street, E C   [One Shilling

"Full of encouragement for the patient townsman who desires a garden or something green to make cheerful his surroundings —*Saturday Review*

THIRD EDITION, REVISED.

THE PERFECT WAY, or, THE FINDING OF CHRIST By ANNA KINGSFORD, M D (Paris), and EDWARD MAITLAND, B.A (Cantab) LONDON The Leadenhall Press Ltd 50, Leadenhall-street, E C   [Seven and Sixpence

---

POLICE ! By CHARLES TEMPEST CLARKSON, thirty three years an Officer of Police, and J HALL RICHARDSON, Journalist on one of the London Dailies. LONDON The Leadenhall Press, Ltd 50, Leadenhall street, E C.   [Six Shillings

Whole page illustrations of Prisoners being photographed for "The Rogues' Gallery", Burglar's Kit, and Metropolitan Police Constable.

THE ROGUES' GALLERY Portraits from Life, of Burglars, Receivers, Forgers, Cracksmen, Smashers, Bank Sneaks, House Thieves, Swell Mobsmen, Pickpockets, Swindlers, and Tricksters. By the Authors of "POLICE!"—C T CLARKSON and J H RICHARDSON Illustrated by HARRY PARKES LONDON The Leadenhall Press, Ltd 50, Leadenhall-street, E C   [One Shilling

---

PRIZE SPECIMENS OF HANDWRITING, LADIES' AND GENTLEMEN'S Contains many specimens, in facsimile, of the best handwriting for which prizes were recently awarded LONDON The Leadenhall Press, Ltd 50, Leadenhall-street, E C   [Sixpence

A SEASON IN EGYPT. By W M FLINDERS PETRIE Illustrated. LONDON. The Leadenhall Press, Ltd 50, Leadenhall street, E.C. [Twelve Shillings.

THE AGE OF MARIE ANTOINETTE A sketch of the period of European revival, which claims amongst its representatives Gœthe, Prudhon, Gainsborough, and Mozart By CHARLES NEWTON SCOTT, author of " The Foregleams of Christianity," &c LONDON The Leadenhall Press, Ltd 50, Leadenhall street, E C [Two Shillings

HOUSEKEEPING MADE EASY. By a Lady. A simplified method of keeping accounts, arranged to commence from any date. LONDON The Leadenhall Press, Ltd 50, Leadenhall street, E C. [One Shilling.

RESCUED ESSAYS OF THOMAS CARLYLE Edited with an Introduction and Notes by PERCY NEWBERRY LONDON The Leadenhall Press, Ltd 50 Leadenhall street, F.C. [Two Shillings.

A PEARL OF ENGLISH RHETORIC
THOMAS CARLYLE ON THE REPEAL OF THE UNION LONDON The Leadenhall Press, Ltd 50, Leadenhall street, L C [Sixpence.

ENGLISH AS SHE IS SPOKE OR A JEST IN SOBER EARNEST Ninth Edition. LONDON · The Leadenhall Press, Ltd 50, Leadenhall-street, E C. [One Shilling.

A manual by means of which the Portuguese author, who has struggled with the difficulties of the English language by aid of dictionary and phrase-book proposes to teach its complexities to his fellow countrymen. The solemn good faith of the writer crowns the unapproachable grotesqueness of his composition.

" Excruciatingly funny "—*The World*

ENGLISH AS SHE IS SPOKE OR A JEST IN SOBER EARNEST " HER SECONDS PART " (new matter) LONDON The Leadenhall Press, Ltd 50, Leadenhall-street, E.C. [One Shilling.

An unlimited mine of salt for diners-out
" Deliciously humorous."—*Detroit Free Press.*

1,000 QUAINT CUTS FROM BOOKS OF OTHER DAYS, including Amusing Illustrations from Children's Story Books, Fables, Chap-books, &c., &c , a Selection of Pictorial Initial Letters and Curious Designs and Ornaments from Original Wooden Blocks belonging to The Leadenhall Press LONDON The Leadenhall Press, Ltd 50, Leadenhall-street, E C. [Sixteen pence

A limited number printed on one side of the paper only at Two-and-Eightpence.

" A wonderful collection of entertaining old wood engravings . . any one of these delights is worth the one and-fourpence." —*Saturday Review.*

If your Stationer does not keep **Stickphast Paste** (**6***d* and **1/-**) he will procure it for you, or we will send a shilling bottle (including strong and useful brush) by Parcel Post on receipt of fifteen stamps. Factory, Sugar Loaf Court, Leadenhall Street, London, E.C.

look how it sticks!

these two sheets of paper
(forming one leaf)
are stuck together
with
Stickphast
Paste

see underneath

(Punch is responsible for this transposition!)

THE
HAIRLESS AUTHOR'S
PAPER PAD.

trs:

"With bad paper, one's best is impossible"

The Author's Hairless Paper-Pad (Issued by The Leadenhall Press, Ltd) Contains, in block form, fifty sheets of strong *hairless* paper, over which—being of unusual but not painful smoothness—the pen slips with perfect freedom Easily detachable, the size of the sheets is about $7\frac{1}{2} \times 8\frac{3}{4}$ in, and the price is only that charged for common scribbling paper. THE AUTHOR'S HAIRLESS PAPER-PAD may be comfortably used, whether at the desk, held in the hand, or resting on the knee. As being most convenient for both author and compositor, the paper is ruled the narrow way, and of course on one side only.— *Sixpence each · 5/- per dozen, ruled or plain.**

The Author's Hairless Paper-Pad Holder— suggested by *Punch*—is equally useful to the busy few who write when travelling, and to stay-at-homes who dislike the restraint of desk or table It is intended that the wooden rim at the side of the AUTHOR'S HAIRLESS PAPER-PAD HOLDER should be grasped by the left hand, the right being free to travel over the whole surface of the paper from top to bottom The height of Pad and Holder will be kept uniform if each written sheet is placed as torn off underneath the Pad, the base of which is now thick blotting paper instead of the old and useless cardboard. The ordinary sloped position when in use keeps Pad and Holder together —*One Shilling each* *

* *If to be forwarded by post, send 2d extra for postage of single Pad and 1s for postage of one dozen Pads The postage on one Pad-Holder is 2d, and one Pad-Holder and one Pad together 3d.*

(15)

Special facilities are possessed for printing *Books, Pamphlets, Prospectuses, Professional and Trading Announcements, &c.,* in that high-class and attractive manner for which THE LEADENHALL PRESS has been so long and favourably known.